KIRSTY MURRAY

A Prayer for
Blue Delaney

CORNELSEN
ENGLISH
LIBRARY

Cornelsen

Cornelsen English Library

Kirsty Murray · A Prayer for Blue Delaney

Kurzfassung
Angela Ringel-Eichinger

Verlagsredaktion
Martin Walsh, Kieran Breen

Umschlaggestaltung
hawemannundmosch, Konzeption und Gestaltung, Berlin

Titelbild
Shutterstock images (© Kitch Bain)

Illustration
Constanze Schargan, Berlin

Gestaltung & technische Umsetzung
Annika Preyhs für Buchgestaltung+

www.cornelsen.de

1. Auflage, 10. Druck 2026

Alle Drucke dieser Auflage sind inhaltlich unverändert
und können im Unterricht nebeneinander verwendet werden.

© 2010 Cornelsen Verlag, Berlin
© 2017 Cornelsen Verlag GmbH, Mecklenburgische Str. 53, 14197 Berlin,
E-Mail: service@cornelsen.de

Druck: H. Heenemann, Berlin

ISBN 978-3-06-032391-3

Contents

*For William Vyvyan Murray
and Rosalind Price
Because music, prayer and the written
word are all acts of faith*

1   A place in the sun

....

Colm took the stairs two at a time, his feet thundering on the dark wood. At the top, he grabbed the balustrade, swung himself into the hall and slid wildly across the wooden floor. His chest ached. The nun was catching up on him, black robes billowing around
5 *her. Any moment now she'd have him.*

'Colm McCabe, stop this instant.' Her voice cut the air like broken glass.

But Colm didn't stop. He kept running, running until the stairs ended and he was at the top of the building, with only the
10 *long, narrow fourth-floor hallway up ahead. That's where Sister Clothilde got him, at the end of the hallway next to the window, where he pressed his hands against the glass and screamed, 'Mum! Mum! Mum!'*

Far below, at the black iron gates of the orphanage, his mother
15 *was leaving. Red hair shone in the morning sunlight, escaping from beneath her blue hat.*

'Mum! Mum! Mum!' he screamed, so loudly that the glass shook. The orphanage echoed with his cries. Sister Clothilde pulled him back along the hallway, hoisted him across her shoulder and
20 *carried him down the long stairs. When she reached the bottom and lowered him to the floor, Colm threw himself against the front door, screaming again for his mother. Someone grabbed him and stuffed something cold and damp into his mouth. Colm tried to spit it out, but the nun put one hand under his chin and held his*
25 *mouth shut.*

'Chew it!'

Colm gagged and tears sprang to his eyes. He was five years old. For the rest of his life, he could never eat potatoes without feeling the cry for his mother that was stopped in his throat.

'What do you know about Australia, lads?' asked a big red-faced man in a dark suit.

No one put up their hand.

'Well, I'll tell you about it. It's a marvellous place. There's kangaroos and horses to ride, and fruit simply falling from the trees. There are families that want boys like you, families with farms where they have their own milk and cream with breakfast every day. No one's ever hungry in Australia. It's a land of plenty and the sun shines every day of the year. So now, who'd like to go to Australia?'

Dibs McGinty's arm shot up. Dozens more followed. Colm kept his hands folded in his lap. Dibs elbowed him sharply. 'Don't you want to get out of this place? Don't you want to ride on a kangaroo?'

'Don't be daft,' whispered Colm. 'You can't ride kangaroos.'

'But we could get away from Sister Clothilde,' said Dibs. 'And we could have families. A real family. A mum, a dad. Maybe even brothers and sisters.'

But still Colm sat with his hands folded in his lap. One day his mother would come back for him and he was going to be waiting for her.

The next day, Sister Clothilde told Colm that he had been chosen.

'Chosen?' he asked.

'For Australia,' she said, pulling her lips back over her teeth and pretending to smile. 'Aren't you lucky?'

'I don't want to go,' said Colm.

'Nonsense. Every boy wants to go. It will be like a grand holiday,' she said, hurrying him outside and shutting the doors of the school behind him.

Colm found Dibs out in the yard. 'I'm going to Australia too,' he said.

Dibs punched him in the arm. 'Good-o. Maybe we'll get adopted by the same family and then we'll be like brothers.'

5 'I'm not getting adopted. I've got a mother already.'

'Well, I am. I'll live in a proper house with a proper mum and dad.'

Colm smiled. Of course, Dibs couldn't remember anything about his mum, so he had to dream of something
10 better.

2 The luck of the Irish

....

The photographer's bulb flashed, and Colm blinked. Everything looked bright and strange – the long line of children marching up the gangway, the crowd on the docks, the steep, grey sides of the ocean liner. Beside him,
5 boys and girls waved at the people on the dockside, though Colm was sure they knew no one down there. They were orphans from all over Britain.

Colm found himself standing in the middle of a group of boys with Irish accents. It made him think of music, the
10 way the words seemed to roll off their tongues. They were bigger than Colm, shouting and laughing as they pushed their way forward to the ship's railing. Colm watched as the tallest of the Irish boys climbed onto the railing, holding onto a post so as not to fall. He was lean and wiry,
15 with a mass of white-blond hair that stuck up in tufts. His friends roared as the boy leant forward and spat as far as he could into the crowd on the docks. A steward yelled from further along the deck and pushed his way towards them. The tall boy turned to jump back on deck, but lost
20 his balance. A gasp rose as he teetered on the railing, his arms flailing wildly. A woman screamed. Instinctively, Colm leapt forward, pushing bodies aside to grab the boy by his shirt and pull him down. They hit the deck together, the big boy landing heavily on Colm.

25 The boy swore and quickly jumped to his feet. Two hands reached down and pulled Colm up.

'You saved me friggin' life, you did,' said the boy in a warm, lilting voice. 'I'm Tommy. Tommy Cassidy from Belfast.' He held his hand out for Colm to shake. The sun shone through his white-gold hair, making a halo of light around his head. Colm put out his hand and felt the older boy's firm handshake. Before Colm could think of anything to say, the steward arrived and angrily pulled Tommy away

5 through the crowd. Tommy looked back, raised one hand to salute and then winked.

The children ran along the decks, laughing and shouting, until three nuns came to take them down to the dining room. Colm slipped between two lifeboats and

10 waited until everyone had gone below decks. When he was alone, he walked to the rail, watching England disappear from view. Inside, he felt a new pain, as if something was being torn away from him as the distance from the shore grew further. He rested his forehead against

15 the railing, humming softly to himself to fight down tears.

Someone put a hand on his shoulder. He looked around to find a small nun standing behind him. A tiny wisp of dark hair had slipped out from under her wimple and it brushed against her smooth round face.

20 'You shouldn't be here, child,' she said.

She turned up the cardboard tag that was pinned to his jacket and nodded.

'Number 49 from St Bartholomew's. You're to be one of my charges during the voyage. You're very lucky to be

25 chosen for such an adventure.'

Colm knew better than to argue with nuns. He let her take his hand and lead him down into the lower part of the ship.

'I'm Sister Mercia. What's your name?'

30 'Colm. Colm McCabe.'

'Well, Colm McCabe, this is the first time I have been to sea and I suspect it is the first time that you have been to sea. I think we should watch out for each other, don't you?'

Colm gazed at her, puzzled. She obviously hadn't been a nun for very long.

5 The third-class dining room was packed with children seated at tables according to the homes they'd come from. Tommy Cassidy was easy to pick out in the crowd with his mass of white-blond hair. Shyly, Colm made his way to Tommy's table.

10 'What are you looking at?' snapped one of the boys.

'Ach, leave off, Paddy, before I have to wipe the table with ye face,' growled Tommy. Then he pushed one of the other boys off the bench and gestured for Colm to sit down.

15 'This is my little mate here, what saved my skin while you idiots stood around with your gobs wide open. There'll be no messin' with him, got that?'

The other boys nodded at Colm.

'Right then,' he said to Colm. 'Tell us your name.'

20 'Colm McCabe.'

Tommy slapped the table hard and laughed. 'So you're Irish. Of course, you had to be Irish – none of the lousy English can think as fast as lads like us.'

Colm had never thought to question whether he was 25 English. Did that mean his mother was Irish too? If Tommy Cassidy was Irish, perhaps it was a good thing to be. Maybe his luck was turning. Maybe this voyage was going to be a grand holiday after all.

....

Blood oozed out of Tommy's thumb and trickled down into his palm. He smiled as he handed the knife to Colm. 'See, nothing to it,' he said.

Colm shut one eye as he slashed the blade across his own thumb.

'Mary, Jesus and Joseph, you didn't need to cut the whole bleeding thing off!' said Tommy, laughing as Colm held one hand beneath the other to catch the blood. Colm grinned, though his hand hurt. Quickly, the two boys pressed their bloodied thumbs together.

'So that's fixed it. We're blood brothers for life,' said Tommy.

'For life,' repeated Colm.

Dibs frowned when Colm explained why he had a handkerchief wrapped around his thumb.

'What you mucking around with that lot for?' he asked as they sat waiting for their turns at badminton.

'I saved Tommy's life, so he says that means that we're joined together forever and we had to do something to prove it. Like in the Westerns, with the Red Indians being blood brothers.'

That night, as Colm lay in his narrow bunk in the cabin, he felt a cloud gather over his thoughts. He gazed out through the porthole at the dark sea. It seemed to be taking a long time to get to Australia. What if his mother came looking for him while they were away? What if a hurricane came and swallowed up the ship with everyone on board?

The questions pounded inside his head until it ached. Colm wished he was back in England.

The next morning, after they'd finished lessons with Sister Mercia, Colm waited until the other children had
5 left the dining hall.

'Sister,' he said, looking at his feet as he spoke, 'do you think we'll be hit by any hurricanes on our holiday?'

Sister Mercia laughed. 'I certainly hope not. But if we do, I'm sure if we pray to our Blessed Virgin Mother, she'll
10 make sure all the orphan children arrive safely in Australia.' She sat down at the piano.

Colm felt his heart lighten. She hadn't said this wasn't a holiday. She hadn't said anything about not going back to England. He moved closer to the piano and when she had
15 finished the piece, he reached out and touched one of the keys.

'Can you play?' asked Sister Mercia.

Colm wanted to laugh, the idea seemed so crazy.

'I always think that, if you're worried about something,
20 playing music can drive all your cares away.'

'I think that too,' said Colm. 'Except all I can do is hum.'

'Well then, hum me a tune and I'll show you how it sounds on the piano.'

Colm hummed 'O for the Wings of a Dove' and Sister
25 Mercia picked out the notes on the piano with her right hand. Colm watched closely. When she'd finished, he asked if he could try. He struggled through the first part of the song. It was much harder than it looked.

'Don't be discouraged, Colm. You're very quick,' said
30 Sister Mercia. 'Perhaps I should teach you. Would you like to have piano lessons?'

Colm looked up into her shining face and tried to smile, fighting back the tears.

'What's the matter, Colm?' she asked,

'I want to go back to England.'

5 'Perhaps, when you grow up, you'll go back for a visit.'

Colm stared at her. 'No. I want to go back now. Sister Clothilde said it would be like a grand holiday. When you go on a holiday, that means you get to go home at the end of it.'

10 Sister Mercia shook her head. 'But Colm, Australia will be our new home.'

Colm looked away from her. How could Australia ever be his home? His home was with his mother.

'Colm,' said Sister Mercia softly. 'Please look at me 15 while I'm talking to you. I have something to tell you. I won't be disembarking in Fremantle. I'm sailing on to Adelaide to join my Order. I'd been saving this to give to you when we reached Australia, but perhaps now is the time for you to have it.'

20 She reached into the folds of her robes and drew out a small card. On one side was a picture of the Virgin Mary in blue robes, with the Baby Jesus in her arms. She was standing in the middle of a brown island in a green sea.

'You see, she's standing in the middle of Australia 25 because she is one of Australia's patrons. I think she should be very special to you, Colm. She's very special to me. Mary is the spiritual mother of all of us. I want you to promise me that whenever you're worried or lonely, you'll pray to her. She is the Queen of Heaven as well as our 30 mother, so she can help you. All you need do is pray to her and she'll hear you.'

Colm fingered the gilt edge of the holy picture. 'My mother wore a blue coat,' he said.

As they entered Fremantle Harbour, the children were all sent to their cabins to put on the good clothes they'd been given before leaving England. Dibs stroked the sleeves of his new blue wool jacket with pleasure, but Colm pulled his clothes on reluctantly. He didn't want to look like the sort of boy someone might want to adopt.

Before they disembarked, Sister Mercia helped them with the navy woollen ties. Colm had never worn one before. As soon as it was pulled tight, he started to sweat. The heat was intense, and the air felt hot.

They walked down the gangway, a long line of pale and excited children. Colm stared out at the docks of Fremantle with despair. Everything was about to change.

There were men with cameras, and people everywhere. Dibs and a little girl in a bright orange dress were chosen to be photographed with an official. The little girl had to hand a bunch of flowers to the wife of the important-looking gentleman while Dibs grinned happily. Colm knew no one would want to take a picture of him. He probably looked too miserable.

When the welcoming session was over and all the officials and cameramen had left, the children were separated like sheep and goats. A Brother in a long dark robe put his hand on the heads of the older boys, directing them to one side. Colm felt his heart sink when Tommy was chosen and separated from him.

4   Dibs adrift

On the bus, Dibs turned to the boy in the next seat. 'Where are they taking us?' he asked. 'Are they taking us to our families?' No one was clear about where they were going.

They drove past a wide blue river and fields of golden
5 grass and orchards of plum trees heavy with fruit. Finally, the bus turned up a long driveway, past a sign that read 'Clontarf, Christian Brothers' Orphanage'.

When they finally disembarked, a small group of boys and two Brothers in black were waiting to show them into
10 the building.

'Will we have to wait long for the parents to come and adopt us?' Colm heard Dibs asking one of the big Australian boys. The boy laughed, and turned to Colm.

'What are you staring at?' the Australian boy asked.
15 'Oi, gooby-eyes. I'm talking to you. What's yer name?'
'That's Colm,' said Dibs.
'Colin?'
'No, Colm.'
'Colm? What sort of a dumb Pommy name is that?'
20 'I'm not a Pommy,' said Colm. 'I'm Irish. My name's McCabe. That's an Irish name.'

'You don't sound like no Irish to me. You sound like a bleeding whinging Pom. Last thing we need around here is another pack of you lot.'
25 The Brothers took away all the clothes the orphan boys had arrived in, including their shoes and their bags, and gave them cotton shorts and shirts to wear instead. Colm managed to keep his picture of Mary by putting it inside his vest, but Dibs wasn't so lucky with his marble collection.

Colm could see he was fighting back tears. The whole time Dibs had been at St Bart's and all through the voyage out, he had guarded his marbles as his most precious possession.

'Excuse me, sir,' said Colm, stepping forward and tapping a Brother on the sleeve. 'Dibs needs to keep his marbles with him.'

The Brother turned. Colm could feel the man's anger. Before Colm could step back, the Brother produced a thick leather belt and strapped Colm across the back of his legs. He shouted at all the boys to get in line, driving them into formation with the strap. As soon as Colm joined the line, the Brother seemed to forget about him.

Colm quickly came to understand that this was no place for asking questions. Every move they made, every breath they took was subject to the discipline of the Brothers in charge of the orphanage. The first few weeks were like running an obstacle course where the boys could only learn by their mistakes what was allowed and what would earn them a flogging with the leather belt.

After they had been there several weeks, Colm discovered that they were allowed to write letters home at weekends, if there was a home to write to. Some of the boys wrote to the Sisters who had run the orphanages that they had come from. But Colm couldn't imagine wanting to write anything to Sister Clothilde. He hoped he'd never see her again. There was only one person in England that Colm wanted to write to. He joined the other boys at the long tables and took the pencil and paper that were offered to him.

'You haven't been in to write a letter home before, McCabe,' said Brother Brophy. 'Have you suddenly thought of someone?'

'I'm going to write to my mother.'

'But the records say your mother is dead.'

'That's a mistake. She's not dead.'

'And where do you expect this letter to be sent to?'

Colm looked up. 'People put messages in bottles, don't they? They put messages in bottles and throw them into the ocean and then people on the other side of the world find them. Maybe someone in the post office will know my mum. Maybe they'll see it and they'll find her for me.'

Brother Brophy opened his mouth to say something but Colm quickly began writing, his head down, the pencil hurrying across the page.

Dear Mum,

I miss you very much. I am at a place called Clontarf in Australia. You can get to Australia on a boat. Please come and find me. I will be a good son. I will be the best son a mother could want.

Love from your boy, Colm McCabe

Colm folded the letter up and placed it in the envelope he'd been provided with. On the front he wrote 'Mrs McCabe, Liverpool, England'. He held the envelope up and stared at it. It didn't look like much of an address but he wasn't sure what else he could write.

That night, as he lay in his narrow bunk, he took out the prayer card of Mary that he kept hidden beneath his mattress. He could just make out the ring of stars around her halo in the moonlight that shone through the dormitory windows. Mary Help of Christians was the Mother of Mercy and the Queen of Heaven. If he asked her, as a mother and a queen, she'd be sure to make Colm's letter reach its destination. He pressed the card against his heart and said a prayer. Now all he had to do was wait.

There were sixty boys in Colm and Dib's classroom, all sitting in rows at old desks. The heat in the room was
5 intense, and when they opened the windows the summer air poured in and made it hotter still. While the Australian boys worked on arithmetic, the migrant boys were given another test. Colm saw Dibs despair at the sight of the questions. Some of the other boys had already been taken
10 out of the classroom and sent to work on the farmland that surrounded the orphanage. If Dibs failed this test, he was sure to be set to work in the fields or orchards and he'd never learn to read and write properly.

Colm finished the paper quickly but he could see that
15 Dibs was struggling, his lips silently mouthing the words, his panic growing more intense as other boys began handing in finished papers. Dibs put his hand up but the teacher didn't notice.

Colm didn't know how to help him. When the bell rang
20 at the end of school, the boys poured out of the classrooms and headed straight to the river to swim. It was one of the few things in the day to look forward to. All the Australian boys swam like fishes. They dived in and quickly reached the deep water in the middle of the wide Canning River.
25 The new boys bathed in a shallow area near the banks. Colm had been practising holding his breath underwater and getting the feel of the water. Today he was ready for more.

Colm wanted to swim out to where he could float
30 alone, staring up at the perfect sky. When the water covered his ears, the rest of the world disappeared. He

turned onto his back and stretched his limbs, imagining he was a small insect, floating on the wide river. Then he became aware of another sound. Someone was calling out. Rolling over, he was startled to see Dibs not far away, thrashing wildly. How on earth had he got there when he couldn't swim?

The distance between himself and Dibs seemed to take forever to cross. By the time he reached the deep water, Dibs had gone under. Colm took a breath and dived down into the cold darkness, until he felt Dibs's head. Reaching deeper, he put one hand under the other boy's arm, pulling him up. Gasping, Dibs immediately tried to climb on top of Colm. He kicked hard to get away, shouting, 'Dibs, don't fight me! You'll drown us both!'

Taking another breath, he swam back but Dibs panicked again, pulling at Colm. Colm punched him then tried to put an arm around Dibs's neck.

Finally, two older boys realised that Colm needed help. They swam in close and helped push Dibs to shallow water and then pulled him up onto the bank. As soon as he touched the dry earth he knelt on his hands and knees, vomiting up water. Slowly, he sat up. Tears streamed from his eyes.

'He tried to drown me,' he sobbed.

'I did not!' said Colm. 'I tried to save you!'

'Not you,' Dibs whimpered. 'Brother Brophy.'

The two older boys looked at each other and raised their eyebrows.

'He was trying to teach you to swim, you Pommy whinger.'

'To drown me,' whispered Dibs.

Colm sat down beside him in a gesture of solidarity against the big Australian boys.

'Don't thank us for saving you, then,' said the older boy.

5 Colm and Dibs said nothing, waiting for the other boys to leave.

'Pommy bastards,' they said, walking away.

Dibs kept on crying hard. Colm rested one hand on Dibs's shoulder and the crying stopped.

10 'He said he was going to take me over the other side,' said Dibs. 'He said, "Put your arms around my neck." And he swam out into the middle of the river and then, when we was in the deep water, he dropped me in the deep water and swam away. If you hadn't come, I'd have
15 drowned.'

Dibs began to cry again. Colm looked out across the shimmering Canning River and imagined floating away under the clear summer sky.

5   The first cut

....

As the wait for a family to adopt him stretched into
months, Dibs seemed to be getting smaller. It was different
for Colm. He had grown taller and stronger since arriving
in Australia, as if the sunshine fed his body and soul. And
5 he was glad no one wanted to adopt him. Every week he
wrote another letter to his mother. Over and over again he
imagined that moment when she would open his letter
and realise that her future was in Australia. Some mornings
he would look down the driveway and almost see her
10 walking along it, her blue coat over her arm, her red hair a
flame against the yellow grass. He was sure she would
come for him.

Sometimes, Colm had to imagine his mother's arrival
over and over again, especially at the end of the day. Every
15 evening, after dinner, was punishment time. Colm
wondered if the Brothers chose that time so the boys
would forget their hunger. They were always hungry.
There was never much food on the table at breakfast,
lunch or dinner. When a boy was called up to be punished,
20 Colm would fold his hands and concentrate extra hard,
trying to think of anything other than what was going on
around him.

The boys were seldom sure why they were being
punished. They only knew it was 'for their own good'.
25 One night, both Colm and Dibs were called up. Everyone
was assembled in the big dining hall to watch.

Brother Brophy stood at the front of the hall, strap in
hand. When Dibs and Colm reached the front of the hall,
he turned them to face the assembly.

'These boys are liars. You are not to believe any of the evil stories they have spread.'

Dibs stood miserably, and Colm started humming to himself.

5 'McGinty, you are an ungrateful, liar. And McCabe, you must know it is a sin to lie. Why did you support McGinty in his lies?'

'I don't know, sir,' said Colm, not looking the man in the eyes. If he could just keep the tune in his mind, he 10 wouldn't notice the pain to come.

'It is our duty to teach you right from wrong. We give you our charity, and you lie in return.'

'Take off your shorts and bend over the chair, McCabe.' Colm bit his lip and heard the strap. His eyes stung as the 15 leather cut his skin. When the sixth blow had fallen, Colm drew his shorts back on. He went back to his place and stared at the dark wood of the table as Dibs stepped up to take his punishment. Dibs was crying even before he had taken his shorts off.

20 'I didn't tell any lies, sir. Please. It was Colm what said you tried to drown me. I know you was trying to teach me to swim. It was Colm. It was Colm who made up the lie.'

Brother Brophy only looked angrier and Dibs cried harder. Suddenly, Colm couldn't bear it. He stood and put 25 his hand up.

'It isn't Dibs's fault, sir. He's right. It's my fault. I started the lie.'

'And why didn't you speak up sooner?' roared Brother Brophy. 'Do you think it's fair to allow McGinty to take 30 punishment for your sins?'

Colm remained silent.

'Speak up!'

'I don't know,' said Colm.

Dibs stood silently all the while, looking from Colm to Brother Brophy.

'Get up here now, McCabe.'

5 Dibs met Colm's eyes for a moment. His face was bright red. Colm wished he could make it clear he didn't mind. It was easier to take another beating than to watch Brother Brophy beat Dibs.

Colm bent over again and waited for the strap to fall.

10 Colm was slow to wake from the nightmare. The first thing he was aware of was the pain in his hand and someone crying out for help. Then he was sitting in Matron's office while she picked pieces of glass from his palm with a pair of tweezers.

15 'What on earth were you thinking, child?' she said as she dropped another sliver of glass into the metal dish beside her.

Colm shrugged and then winced at the pain.

'I don't remember.'

20 He did remember the dream, but it wasn't something he would tell her about. It was the same dream that he'd had since he was six – the dream that always sent him sleepwalking. It always happened when it rained.

It was raining now. The sound of the rain on the roof
25 was a rhythmic thrumming, the first Colm had heard since he'd arrived in Australia. When he lay down in his narrow bed, he tried to hold those thoughts of his mother, but instead he could only see Dibs's startled face – Dibs adrift in the dark waters of the Canning River, while all his hopes
30 and dreams were swept away by the current.

6 Bindoon

Colm stood by the roadside with a small group of boys. He wasn't sure if it was because they thought he was a liar or because he broke the dormitory window, but he was being sent to another orphanage. But wherever they were
5 sending him now, it couldn't be worse than Clontarf.

When Colm had told Dibs he was being sent away, Dibs had said nothing, expressing neither interest, disappointment nor shame. Colm felt a flash of anger. It was in that moment that Colm realised Dibs wasn't the
10 boy he used to know.

The truck drove through the pale gold countryside. Then they turned off the main highway and down small roads cut into red, red soil. Colm laughed out loud when they passed through the main gates of Boys' Town and he
15 saw the name of the orphanage: Bindoon. Tommy had been sent to Bindoon. He was going to be with Tommy again. He knelt on his seat and pressed his face against the bus window, smiling at every tree and stone.

Along the roadside stood small mounds of rock with
20 pictures on them. It wasn't until they'd driven past several that Colm realised they showed the Stations of the Cross. Catching a glimpse of Mary and Jesus on the fourth Station, he touched the prayer card in his pocket. He'd only just had time to rescue it from beneath his mattress
25 before they left. The gilt was wearing off the edges but Mary's face still looked calm and the Baby Jesus had lost none of his freshness, even if it was a little crumpled. As long as he had the prayer card, Colm knew his hopes and dreams might still come true.

At the bottom of the hill were the main buildings, like a mass of Spanish-looking castles with towers and porticos. As they drew closer, Colm could see that the buildings were still incomplete. There were building materials everywhere. Colm jumped out of the truck. A group of small boys watched the new arrivals with no interest. Then three figures came trudging along a road from the green hills. Colm recognised Tommy, even before he could see his face, from the way he moved and the mass of his white-blond hair. It was shorter and even whiter than when Colm had seen him get into the truck at the docks in Fremantle.

Colm ran to meet him.

'Tommy, Tommy,' he called, breathless with excitement. Tommy stopped. 'What are you doing here?'

'Aren't you glad to see me?'

'No. You don't want to be here, mate. This place, this is hell.'

Colm looked to the green-and-gold countryside, and the dam lying in the sunlight, and stared back at Tommy, not understanding.

'Nothing's the way it looks from the outside,' said Tommy.

He said nothing more until they reached the boys' home. Two Brothers in black were driving the new boys up the steps of the building. Colm slipped his hand into his pocket and touched Mary Help of Christians.

That afternoon, some official visitors called on the orphanage, and Tommy and two other boys were asked to sing for them.

'Do you sing, Tommy?' asked Colm.

'Bloody hate it. Old Keaney makes us sing for the visitors. Wants to show off what a marvellous bloody job he's doing. Bastard.'

'It can't be that bad. I don't mind singing. I'd go in your place.'

Tommy laughed. 'I wouldn't want you to go. Couldn't do that to a mate. We get beaten with his stick before we start and beaten again when we're done, 'cause we're never good enough. And if we sing a wrong note, he hits us then, too. You're well out of it.'

In the evening, Tommy and the other Northern Irish boys were made to stand on a table in the dining room and sing for Brother Keaney again. Some of the other boys laughed at them. Colm sat uncomfortably on the hard bench. He could hear the misery in their voices and it made something ache deep inside him.

That night in the crowded dormitory, Colm lay looking up at the high roof. Boys crying in their sleep kept him awake long into the night. It was nearly six months since he'd left Liverpool. He counted up the weeks and months, trying to calculate when his mother might have got his letters. What if she went to Clontarf and didn't find him? Surely they'd tell her he was here at Bindoon. Maybe if she came, she would take Tommy away as well. Colm pulled out his prayer card and pressed it against his chest, praying to Mary to guide his mother to him.

The next morning after mass, some of the boys went to the dining hall to write letters home. Colm went to follow them, but Tommy grabbed his arm.

'Where you going?' he asked.

'I've been writing to my mum every weekend. I have to tell her I'm at Bindoon now. One day, she's going to come and take me away.'

Tommy laughed, but it was more like a bark than a
5 happy sound. 'Don't go wasting your time. She won't be coming for you. Not if it's the letters that you think is bringing her.'

'Yes she will,' said Colm.

'Look, lad,' said Tommy, putting a hand on Colm's
10 shoulder. 'They don't send your letters nowhere. I was moving cupboards a while back. Found a whole pile of boys' letters fallen down behind them. They're not gonna waste good pennies on postage for us lot.'

Colm stood on the steps of the chapel and felt darkness
15 come down on him. By the banks of the dam, families were enjoying Sunday picnic lunches. The Brothers encouraged families to visit the grounds of Bindoon so the world could see the good work they were doing, but the boys were not allowed to speak to the picnickers. Now
20 Colm stared at these people, wanting to shout at them, wanting to tell them that nothing was as it seemed.

Some of the boys who had come from Clontarf seemed to think that Bindoon would be a holiday. But on Monday morning, all the boys started work. Colm didn't care.
25 Anything that kept him from thinking about the dark future was a good thing. And at least he was working with Tommy.

The new boys were set to work alongside boys who could teach them what to do. Colm's job was to help
30 concrete the floor of the entrance to the main building. He and Tommy worked on their hands and knees.

The concrete was rough against Colm's skin but the work was rhythmic. As he slapped the concrete down, he hummed the melancholy song that Tommy had sung last night. He had just reached the chorus when a boot kicked
5 him so hard that he landed face first in the wet concrete.

'You're learning a job. There's nothing for you to be singing about,' shouted Brother Keaney. The song froze in the back of Colm's throat. He had to shade his eyes against the bright sunlight as he looked up at Brother Keaney's
10 mass of hair, white against the blue sky.

Colm was made to stay concreting until the portico entrance was finished, even after the dark night came down around him. Every hour a Brother would come to check on him and tell him to keep at it. The moon rose and
15 shone down brighter than the dim lamp that lit Colm's work. When he'd finally reached the top of the steps, Brother Dennis came to tell him he could go to bed.

'Can I wash the concrete off, please, sir? It hurts my skin.'

20 The Brother looked at Colm for a long moment. 'Come with me,' he said.

In his long black robes the Brother looked like a dark spirit as he walked in and out of the shadows of the building. Colm was so tired, so hungry and sore, that he
25 could barely keep up with him. They were halfway across the yard when a wiry figure came running towards them and knocked straight into Colm. He fell to the ground.

Brother Dennis grabbed both boys and pulled them to their feet. He shook the other boy violently by his
30 shoulders. It was Tommy.

'What do you think you're doing?' he barked.

'Just coming back from Brother Keaney, sir,' said Tommy. 'He asked for me. To warm his bed, like. And then I saw you and thought I'd show McCabe the way back to the dormitory, sir. Save you the trouble.'

Brother Dennis looked from Tommy to Colm. Before he could say anything else, Tommy grabbed Colm by the arm. 'Run!' he whispered into Colm's ear.

They ran towards the boys' dormitory.

In the shadow of the portico, they stopped to catch their breath and watched as Brother Dennis disappeared into the Brothers' building.

'Why did we have to run?' whispered Colm.

'You don't want to get yourself alone with Brother Dennis, not at night, when no one knows where you are. Believe me.'

'Why not? And why were you warming Brother Keaney's bed?'

'The old git makes us lie at the end of the bed so he can warm his feet. Then, when he's snoring, we get out. You was lucky he fell asleep when he did so that I could rescue you.'

'I wanted to wash this concrete off,' said Colm.

'You should be thanking me, not worrying about washing. I'll cop it tomorrow for getting in Dennis's way.'

Suddenly, through the shadows, they saw a movement in the moonlit yard. Brother Dennis was heading straight towards the boys' dormitory entrance. Tommy pulled Colm back into the shadows.

'Sweet Jesus. What if he doesn't wait until tomorrow? He knows where I sleep.' Tommy jumped nervously from one foot to the other, talking fast in a low whisper. 'Listen, I'm getting out of here, Colm. I'm not waiting for whatever he wants to do with me. I'm sick of this place, sick of the work and the beatings and being old Keaney's whipping boy. I asked him once, I said, "You're Irish and we're Irish. Why are you so hard on us?" And you know what he said? He said, "You are the son of a whore." That's what they think of us. They think we're sons of whores. That Brother Dennis, he's already tried to touch me once. I'm not giving him a second chance. I'm thirteen now. Old enough to make me own way.'

'Let me come too,' said Colm.

'You're still too little. They'll catch you for sure. Quick, get yourself in bed, down with the Clontarf boys. I'll go north and find myself work, be a jackeroo. That's what they call cowboys in this country. If I go now, I'll have a whole night's start on them.'

They waited in the dark until Brother Dennis came out of the dormitory again and returned to his room. 'Here's my chance,' said Tommy. 'So long'

Colm grabbed his hand in a last grip and they pressed their thumbs together so the scars of their blood brotherhood touched. 'Keep safe.'

Tommy rushed into the scrub, his hair shining in the moonlight, and Colm walked into the dormitory alone.

Colm tiptoed down the length of the room until he came to the row of camp beds set up for the Clontarf boys. Exhaustion overcame him as soon as he lay down. The last thing he saw was a black shadow in the doorway of the dormitory. All night he dreamt of running with Tommy by his side.

7 The broken boy

The next morning, Tommy was gone. Colm was called up for questioning, but to every question he simply answered, 'I don't know.'

As soon as the interview was over, Colm was sent back
5 to work. Thousands of people were going to come to admire the orphanage at an 'open day' next week and nothing was ready. Everyone had to work fast, faster than they ever had before. Maybe it was a good time for Tommy to have run away. Surely the Brothers would be too busy
10 to go looking for him.

But that afternoon, Brother Dennis drove back into Boys' Town with a crumpled figure seated beside him in the front of the orphanage truck. Colm looked up from where he was working on the verandahs and felt his heart
15 grow cold. Something about the way Tommy was sitting in the seat made him feel afraid.

When Tommy climbed out of the truck, he stumbled like an old man. Then he fell. Brother Dennis stood over him, talking in a low, angry tone.

20 'Get up, get up,' whispered Colm, willing Tommy to get to his feet. But Tommy started to crawl on hands and knees, as if he had lost all sense of who he was. Brother Dennis grabbed him roughly by one arm, pulled him to his feet and led him towards the building.

25 No one saw Tommy again until after teatime. He came into the dormitory as the boys were climbing into bed and limped between the rows of bunks with his gaze fixed on the floor. The usual noise of bedtime was silenced. All his thick, white hair was gone, shaved off. One eye was

swollen shut, and when he lay down on his bunk it was as if every movement caused extreme pain.

Colm and several of Tommy's friends gathered around him.

5   'Tommy,' said Colm, reaching out to touch him on the shoulder.

Tommy winced.

'I haven't seen a boy have his head shaved for a while,' said one of the older boys. 'The brothers must have been
10 really angry with him. Did they beat you hard, Tommy?'

Tommy lay silent. Gently, Colm raised the back of Tommy's shirt to see how bad the damage was. His back was a mass of red welts, raw and swollen. Colm felt sick.

In the morning, Tommy wouldn't eat his gruel. Colm
15 felt a tight knot form in his stomach.

'Tommy,' he whispered. 'You have to try to eat. They'll beat you again if you don't.'

Tommy looked at him with a stranger's eyes.

Colm checked that no one was watching and then
20 quickly scraped Tommy's breakfast into his own bowl and wolfed down the gruel. He felt guilty, but he knew that Tommy couldn't stand another beating.

Out in the bright sunshine, they were marched up to the grand new building to begin working on the walls on
25 the second floor. Brother Keaney came towards them, shouting up at the boys, 'Wake up and get working.' Tommy didn't move, staring into space.

Colm scrambled over to Tommy and grabbed his arm.

'Please, Tommy, wake up!'

30 Brother Keaney shouted for Tommy and Colm. He looked Tommy up and down. 'Not up to much today, are you, Cassidy? That'll teach you to run away. Here, Sullivan

and you, whatever your name is, take Cassidy down to the dam. The super bags need washing.'

Colm took Tommy's arm and guided him down the steps, following Sullivan. Beside the vegetable gardens was a small cart and a pile of old bags smelling of superphosphate.

'Right then,' said Sullivan. 'You done this before?' Colm shook his head and looked to Tommy, but Tommy stood silent.

'Well,' said Sullivan, 'We have to load up the bags and take 'em down the dam to wash. Then we hang 'em on the fence to dry. You and me, we'll be like the donkeys and pull the cart, and Tommy, he can push from behind.'

Colm and Sullivan worked quickly, but Tommy struggled to lift even a single bag. Sullivan looked at Tommy and shook his head. 'Here, why don't you ride on the cart and me and Colm will pull you down to the dam?' he said.

Silently, Tommy climbed on top of the bags while Colm and Sullivan pushed it down to the dam. It took them over an hour to clean the stinking bags and load them back onto the cart. Colm tried to get Tommy talking, but he didn't answer. When they'd finished, Tommy climbed back into the cart and lay on top of the wet bags.

Sullivan and Colm started to drag the cart uphill. The weight of the wet bags and the hill made it difficult work.

'Here, this is no good. He'll have to jump down and help us,' said Sullivan.

'No, I'll get behind and push. Give me a minute.' Colm hurried to the back of the cart, but they had only pushed it a metre when he stumbled. Sullivan let out a shout and suddenly the cart was rolling backwards.

Colm saw the wheels roll past his shoulder. Sullivan shouted, 'Jump, Tommy! Jump clear!'

Colm got to his feet and saw the cart rushing down the hill towards the dam with Tommy on top. Colm ran, but he couldn't catch up. The cart hit a rock and overturned, throwing Tommy to the ground. He lay beneath the cart, blood oozing from his shaved head, forming a dark puddle in the red dirt.

'Tommy, Tommy!' cried Colm again and again as he and Sullivan threw themselves against the cart and desperately tried to pull it away. Finally, Sullivan stuck a piece of wood under the cart while Colm dragged Tommy's body free.

Colm held Tommy against him. It was like holding a weak animal, as if all the energy that was in Tommy had disappeared. Blood covered Colm's hands.

'Get help,' he said to Sullivan. 'Get help, quickly.'

'I can't go quick, it's my foot. You're fast, I seen you. You go,' said Sullivan, kneeling down beside him.

'I'll stay with Tommy.'

The red dirt flew as Colm raced up the hill towards Boys' Town, running faster than he had ever run in his life.

8 Nothing to lose

They laid Tommy's body on a table between the chapel and the dining room. The story spread like wildfire. Tommy Cassidy is dead. The words echoed in Colm's head, but they made no sense. He had run as fast as he could. He had
5 prayed with all his heart, pressing the holy card between his hands as he begged Blessed Mary to save Tommy. But Tommy had died anyway.

That evening, Colm couldn't face the meal. The steam from the dark tea smelt bitter. He kept his head down,
10 staring into his lap where his hands lay, formed into two fists.

When Brother Dennis came into the dining room, Colm wasn't the only boy not eating. Brother Dennis walked between the tables, hitting those who had food left on
15 their plates with his belt until they hurriedly reached for their spoons. Some boys wept as they ate, but Colm wouldn't cry. He pushed the plate away and sat, staring at his fists, feeling his own rage burning inside him. When Brother Dennis stopped by his place, he grabbed a fistful of
20 potato and threw it into Brother Dennis's face. The dining hall fell silent. Brother Dennis wiped his cheeks. He was trembling with rage. Colm couldn't help but gasp as the man dragged him from the dining hall by his hair.

Colm didn't cry once as the belt cut again and again,
25 tearing his skin. When it was over, he pulled on his shorts and shirt in silence and stumbled to the dormitories.

That night, after everyone in Boys' Town was asleep, Colm climbed out of his narrow bed. Moonlight lit the path to the small graveyard where they had buried Tommy that afternoon. He looked at the wooden cross that marked the grave, hating the thought of Tommy beneath the dirt. He knelt down, took out his prayer card of Mary Help of Christians and placed it at the foot of the cross. Now that Tommy was in heaven, he was with her. If Tommy had a mother, she would never see him again.

Colm knew now what he had to do. He didn't care about the risks, he had to get away. He had nothing to take with him and nothing to lose. Somehow, some way, he was going to get back to his mother.

Barefoot, his body hurting from Brother Dennis's thrashing, he took the road away from Bindoon. The moon shone bright on the Stations of the Cross. At the fifth Station he knelt down beside the picture of Simon of Cyrene carrying the cross for Christ. He felt as if he was dragging a cross right now, and he fought back tears with every step. At last, Colm turned onto the long moonlit road that led to Perth and Fremantle.

He walked all night until his feet were sore and when dawn came he turned off the road and lay down in the long yellow grass. He woke in the early afternoon. His feet were hurting and he wondered how he would make it all the way to Fremantle on foot. Maybe he should try to hitch a ride? But then if someone picked him up, they might take him back. Back to Brother Dennis. He started humming loudly at the thought, but there was no song loud enough to drown his fears of the man. He began thinking what he'd do when he got to Fremantle. He would find a big ship and hide on it. If that was the only way to get back to his mother, then he was prepared to do it. Having a plan gave him the strength to keep moving.

For the rest of the afternoon he limped along the dusty roadside, hiding in the grass whenever a truck or car came in view. His ears became used to the soft rumble of vehicles coming nearer but he was startled when a bike stopped
5 beside him. There was nowhere to hide. 'Hello there,' said the rider, a young brown-eyed man.

Colm didn't reply.

'You one of those kids from Boys' Town? Those shorts and shirt are a giveaway, mate. Orphan clothes. What you
10 doing wandering so far from home?'

Colm looked up then and stared hard into the man's face. 'I'm going home. To my mum,' he said firmly.

'Well, you've a long way to go. Jump on. I'll take you as far as Bullsbrook East. You've got a long walk to Perth. Is
15 that where your mum is?'

'Fremantle, I have to get to Fremantle,' said Colm, getting onto the front of the bicycle.

The young man took Colm to the intersection of the highway and a dusty track that led to his family's farm.

20 'Now don't you try walking all the way to Fremantle,' he advised. 'You've got more than fifty miles to go and you can't do that without shoes. Early tomorrow morning, there'll be farmers taking fruit down to the Fremantle markets. You hitch a ride with one of them.'

25 He waved and pedalled away.

In the afternoon, the heat was so intense that all he could do was lie in the shade of a tree with his arms over his eyes and wait. That night he walked for hours in the darkness. Anything was better than lying alone in the
30 black countryside. In the early dawn, a truck came down the road. Colm stood behind a tree and watched it pass. It hit a bump and something flew out of the back. When the

truck was far from view, Colm discovered the something was a peach, damaged but good enough to eat. The juice burned his throat but stopped his thirst.

It was two days and another long night of walking
5 before he found the courage to hitch a ride with the morning fruit trucks. There was no room in the cab with the driver and his mate, so they let Colm climb up in the back with crates of apricots. They weren't quite ripe, but Colm didn't care. He sucked the sour juice as he lay amidst
10 the boxes. Soon he'd be in Fremantle, soon he'd be on his way home to his mother.

9 Acts of faith

Colm felt weak with hunger but he trudged on, determined to follow his plan. He walked along the docks, staring up at the huge ocean liners. One of those ships had to be going back to England. But how was he going to get on board?
5 Most of them were moored some distance from the docks. Even if he could swim out to them, it would be impossible to climb on board. His head ached. He pressed his fists against his forehead, trying to organise his thoughts.

An old man was sitting on the edge of the dock with a
10 fishing line, his dog lying sleepily beside him. He drank from a bottle and then poured some water into a dish for the dog. Colm licked his lips as he watched the old dog drinking up the water.

The brilliant sun on the sea made Colm's head hurt. He
15 sat down and put his head in his hands.

He felt something cold and wet against his feet. The fisherman's dog sat in front of him, staring with serious brown eyes. Unsure, Colm stroked the dog on its head, expecting it to walk away. But the dog had other ideas. It
20 dropped its head and began licking Colm's bare feet. Colm pulled them away but the dog carried on, licking the dust and dried blood. The softness of the dog's tongue against his aching feet was strangely soothing. He moved his toes and the dog licked those as well. Even though it hurt his
25 chest to laugh, Colm giggled, and the dog sat down beside him as though they were old friends. Colm ran one hand along its red coat. It looked like a working dog, the sort of dog farmers kept to round up sheep and cattle. Its tail swung lazily backwards and forwards as he stroked its fur.

After a while, Colm lay back against the statue again, enjoying the closeness of the animal. He closed his eyes. When he opened his eyes again he saw the old fisherman standing in front of him.

5   'She bothering you?' the man asked, pointing at the dog.

Colm shook his head.

'Funny, that. She doesn't usually like strangers. One-man dog, my Rusty. She must have felt sorry for you. You
10 look done in, mate.'

He pulled a glass bottle of orange drink out of his leather bag and offered it to Colm. It was warm and fizzy.

'You can keep it.'

'Thank you,' said Colm.

15 The man picked up his bucket and leather bag. 'C'mon, Rusty,' he said. 'Time to hit the frog and toad.'

The dog opened one eye and didn't move.

'Rusty,' said the man again, more firmly.

Reluctantly, the old dog got to its feet and stretched.
20 Then it pressed its head into Colm's chest, as if to say goodbye. The old man looked at Colm.

'You been feeding her?' he asked, a trace of annoyance in his voice.

Colm shook his head again. 'But she licked my toes.'

25 'Licked your toes?' repeated the man, astonished. He tipped his hat back and shook his head. 'Damn dog. Getting old, she is. Reckon she's getting confused about … well, about strangers.'

Colm scratched Rusty behind the ear. He wished the
30 man would go away and leave the dog behind, but instead, the old man sat down beside Colm.

'Mind if I join you?' he asked.

He looked at Colm with sharp blue eyes and said, 'Here, why aren't you in school? '

Colm got to his feet, wincing.

'I'm going home. Home to England.'

5 'You're not thinking of hiding on one of these ships?'

Colm didn't answer. He didn't want to tell his story. He felt the man was laughing at him.

'It's not a joke,' he said angrily.

'I wasn't laughing. A long time ago, I stood on a dock,
10 just like you, looking for a boat to hide on. I remember, I was hungry, walking up and down that dock. I was heading south, though, not to the land of Poms, like you. You shouldn't be wanting to go back to England. It's a hole. Boy like you can have a future here.'

15 Colm thought of the boys at Bindoon, and of Tommy who had no future. Again, he saw Tommy lying on the table outside the dining room.

'Here, you all right?' asked the old man.

Colm felt as if the man could see straight through him.

20 'I've got some biscuits and a thermos of sweet tea. You reckon you can stop a while before you find that ship? Have a bit of tucker?'

Colm nodded. The man pulled out his thermos and a biscuit wrapped in paper.

25 Colm had never thought a biscuit and tea could taste so good. They sat silently staring over the blue water at the ocean liners sailing in and out of the harbour.

'So what's your name?' asked the man.

Colm started stroking the dog again, pretending that he
30 hadn't heard.

The old man looked at him. 'Well, I'm Bill Dare and this here dog is my old mate, Rusty.' He stroked the kelpie between the ears. 'You can call me Bill.'

Colm kept his eyes fixed on the water.

5 'Look, Sonny Jim, I know hiding on a ship sounds like a big adventure, but I think it's about time you thought about getting home.'

'Don't have a home. Only the boys' home. Never going back there. Never.'

10 Bill rested his hand on Colm's shoulder.

Colm stood up and took a few steps. He bent to stroke the old kelpie, to say goodbye, but Rusty had other ideas. As soon as Colm stopped, she started licking his feet again.

'Sweet Jesus,' said Bill. 'Your feet …' He picked up his 15 bucket and leather bag in one hand and then gestured to Colm to follow him. 'Come on. You don't want to run any further on them. Rusty knows her business. You come along with us.'

Colm put his hands over his face and tried to hum 20 something, anything that would make his mind clear.

'Oi, little mate,' said Bill, his voice quiet and calm. 'I won't give you away. Come on back to my place. Just until you get back on your feet. If you hang about here on the docks, someone will catch you and take you back to that 25 boys' home. You don't want that.'

Rusty and Bill watched him, waiting for his answer. Slowly, he nodded.

They walked through the streets of Fremantle. Colm kept his eyes on the ground, afraid to look up in case he 30 saw a policeman and gave himself away. They passed by a prison with high walls and a ring of barbed wire around the top. Colm thought of Bindoon. He hadn't had to climb over high walls and barbed wire to escape, but it had still been a prison.

The walk to Bill's home seemed to take a long time. Finally, they came to a door in a long wall. The old man took an old-fashioned key out of his pocket, and unlocked the big black door. It opened on to a courtyard with tall palms. On the other side, through two more thick black doors, was the entrance to an old stone building. They passed down a narrow hall into a long room with windows high in the wall. There were boxes and bits and pieces around the big open fireplace, and two beds against one wall.

'Is this a prison?' asked Colm, warily.

'I suppose it was, once. Used to be a nut-house, Fremantle Asylum for the Insane. But there's only me these days.'

For a moment, Colm felt panic. He didn't know this man and now they were locked inside an insane asylum together. Bill laughed.

'Don't worry, I'm not crazy. I'm the caretaker here. There's no more crazy people here any more. You sit yourself down. We need to put something on those feet of yours.'

Colm sat on a box in the middle of the room while Bill gently washed his feet. The medicine stung but it was a good sort of pain, a pain that meant things were going to get better. When he'd finished, the old man took out a piece of clean white bandage and wrapped it around Colm's feet. He warmed up a tin of rice pudding and pushed it towards Colm.

'Eat up,' he said. 'Reckon you need something like this to stick to your ribs.'

Colm thought he'd never tasted anything so delicious in all his life. It was warm and sweet and it made him want to cry.

Then he lay down beside Rusty on one of the narrow bunks. Afternoon sunlight shone through the high windows, but Colm was asleep in a moment, his body close to the old kelpie, his thoughts slipping into gentle dreams.

....

When Colm woke, a soft pink light was shining in through the windows.

'Morning, sonny,' said the old man.

'Morning?' echoed Colm.

5 'You've been asleep fifteen hours, near enough. Must have needed it.'

Bill sat on the edge of the other bunk, putting on his shoes, and then he put on a blue jacket. Rusty watched him, wagging her tail with excitement.

10 'We're going down to catch the morning tide, see if we can catch us something to eat.'

Colm struggled to sit up but as his feet met the floor he felt sick.

'No, you're not coming with us, mate. You were real 15 sick during the night, calling out in your sleep. Reckon, you've still got a bit of a temperature. You rest. When I come back, we'll have a talk about what's to become of you.'

Colm felt his chest grow tight. Was Bill planning to 20 hand him over to the police? He was uncomfortably aware that he was at the mercy of this old man. He listened to Bill's footsteps going down the passage.

He climbed out of bed and winced as his feet touched the wooden floorboards. A wave of sickness took hold of 25 him. If he could see the sky, he thought, then perhaps it wouldn't feel so scary inside the old asylum.

The stairs were old, and he had to walk carefully. From a small window at the top, he could see Bill and Rusty walking down the road towards Fremantle. Suddenly he

felt as if he was falling – that he would fall straight through the glass and into the street below. He shut his eyes. Inside his head, he could hear a voice, as if someone was calling him, looking for him. His legs collapsed and as he fell, he
5 heard a woman crying, then the sound of breaking glass.

Colm was vaguely aware of firm hands guiding him back down the stairs and into the caretaker's rooms.

'What were you doing, mate?' said Bill. 'How long were you lying there? You can't go walking around the place
10 like that.'

'I heard someone, she was looking for me. A woman calling me,' he said in a small voice.

'That must have been Ethel. She was brought here – mad with grief after someone kidnapped her girl. She
15 jumped out one of the first-floor windows. Reckon it was that window I found you lying under. Some folk reckon she still walks the passageways, searching for her daughter. Poor old thing.'

Colm had never thought about that before, that a
20 mother might go mad with grief at the loss of her child. Thoughts of his own mother came back, and he wished he could stop feeling sick.

'Ethel's the least of your worries around here, though. Lucky you didn't bump into Moondyne Joe. Mad old
25 bushranger that died here in 1900. Now, let's get you out of that outfit of yours. I should have sorted some jim-jams for you last night. Been a long time since I've had a kid around.'

Then Bill lifted Colm's shirt, and his face turned pale.
30 'Here, what's all this?' He held Colm by the shoulders and looked at his back.

Colm didn't answer. He could still hear the cries of the woman echoing in his mind. He saw Bill staring at his back where Brother Dennis's strap had cut deep. It felt as though the wounds were oozing pus. Then he passed out.

5   When Colm woke again, there was a gold patch of late-afternoon sunlight lying on the floor. Bill sat next to the bed and a man in black stood over Colm.

The stranger was taking things out of a leather bag.

'You may think it's harsh, Bill. On the one hand, I agree
10 with you, but on the other hand you don't know this boy. He could be a bad one. You don't know what he did to deserve the beating. Those Brothers are working hard to make men of these boys. Why, at Clontarf there are over 200 boys and only six brothers. It's no surprise they have
15 to use the strap.'

'I don't care what his crime was. I've never held with beating little ones, and even if I did, no child deserves to be thrashed like that. God knows how he made it to Fremantle. He's got guts, this one. Didn't breathe a word
20 to me about the beating. It was only when I found him at the top of the stairs, passed out cold, that I realised there was something wrong.'

The doctor bent over Colm and examined his cuts. 'Some of these are infected. There's not much meat on his
25 bones, is there?'

Colm turned and stared up at the doctor.

'You're awake are you, young man? Can you sit up for me?'

The doctor listened to his chest, looked down his throat
30 and in his ears. 'I'll give him some penicillin and send a car around to collect him later this afternoon. I can't take him now,' he said to Bill.

Bill nodded and Colm felt panic rise up.

As soon as the doctor was gone, Colm swung his feet over the side of the bed and tried to stand.

'Can't go back,' he said, struggling to speak. 'Brother
5 Dennis will kill me.' Bill stared at him.

'The Brothers might beat you, mate, but they wouldn't murder you.'

Colm fell to the floor, kneeling in front of Bill, his hands folded in prayer. 'Please,' he said, 'please. Don't let them
10 take me back.'

Rusty jumped down from her place on the end of Bill's bed and Colm pressed his face into her dusty fur. At least Rusty understood.

'Jesus, Mary and Joseph. What shall I tell the doctor?'
15 said Bill.

Later that day, Colm lay with Rusty beside him, and listened to Bill tell the doctor's driver that the boy had run away again and he didn't know where he was.

It took days for Colm to feel strong enough to leave his
20 bed. On the evening of his first day up, Bill lit a fire in the courtyard. He opened a tin of baked beans to heat in a black billycan and cooked sausages over the flames on a long fork.

Bill looked at him across the flames. 'Good to see you
25 up and about, cobber. But you're going to have to keep a low profile. I ran into Doctor Do-gooder down at the pub. If he sees you walking around Fremantle, he'll be after you.'

Colm stopped eating and stared miserably into the
30 flames.

'Don't worry,' said Bill. 'You can hide out here until you feel strong again. That is, if you don't mind an old man, a dog and a few ghosts for company.'

It wasn't hard for Colm to keep hidden. No one came to
5   visit Bill's corner of the asylum. It was strange having whole days to himself with nothing much to do. One day he found an old piano in the dining hall. From then on, he would sit at the piano every day and practise the tunes that Sister Mercia had taught him over and over again.
10 Sometimes Rusty sat beside him, her head on one side, as if she enjoyed the concert.

As the weeks went on, Colm's life found a rhythm again. During the morning he'd play the piano or read newspapers or an old Bible that he'd found on the second
15 floor. Sometimes he'd help Bill with tasks around the asylum, sweeping the courtyard or holding a piece of wood while Bill hammered it into place. In the evening, Bill would ask him to read out loud while he cooked their dinner. Bill wasn't much of a cook, but there was never a
20 shortage of beans and sausages and sometimes he'd bring a parcel of fish and chips with him when he came back from an afternoon down in Fremantle. Slowly Colm's wounds began to heal until there were only scars on his back.

One morning while Bill and Rusty were out, Colm sat
25 in the courtyard reading the newspapers and saw that the Queen of England was travelling around Australia, visiting towns and cities all over the country. Every day there was more about the royal visit, and special pictures celebrating her Australian tour. But now she was coming to Fremantle.
30 Colm carefully tore out the picture of her coronation and put it under his pillow.

That night he dreamt about a queen. He wasn't sure whether it was the Queen of Heaven or the Queen of England. But the queen in his dream was holding the hand of a boy, a smiling boy with white-blond hair. Colm woke, Tommy's name on his lips. Was Tommy trying to send him a message? Why was Tommy with the Queen? Was she his mother now? Colm knew the dream was trying to tell him something, but he couldn't understand what it was.

The next day, Colm read out some of the news about the arrival of the Queen while Bill made toast. There was an outbreak of polio in Western Australia and all the plans for the royal visit had to be changed. The royal ship, the *Gothic,* had been moored off Fremantle. There were lots of warnings advising people to avoid large groups for fear of the polio epidemic spreading, but thousands of people were expected at the dock to see her disembark and drive to the airport for her flight back to Britain.

'Do you think maybe we could go down to the docks?' asked Colm. 'It could be our last chance.'

'Daft idea,' said Bill grumpily. 'You don't want to get mixed up in that crowd. There'll be policemen all over the place.'

Colm said, 'I'd risk it for her. She's our Queen.'

'She's not *my* bloody Queen. This bloody country should have been a republic years ago. You won't see me going down to stare at her and her husband.'

Colm didn't bother to argue any further. He folded up the newspaper and began playing a tune on the old piano. As he played, he thought about the *Gothic* sailing home. A boat sailing to England with no passengers on board. Suddenly, Colm started to understand what his dream might have been trying to tell him.

11   Bitter truth

....

The morning that the Queen was to leave Fremantle, Colm waited until Bill and Rusty had gone out, then he opened the courtyard doors and stepped out into the street.

It was strange to be outside after the weeks shut up in
5 the asylum. Whenever a car drove past, he found it hard not to jump behind a fence to hide. As he walked down the hill towards the docks, he took a deep breath and smelt the sea breeze. It smelt like freedom. But when he turned out of a narrow road into one of the main streets of
10 Fremantle, Colm realised he'd made a mistake. The roads were full of cars and people heading for the docks, and just as Bill had said, there were policemen everywhere. No one seemed to be worried about the risk of catching polio. Pushing between a tall man in a dark suit and his well-
15 dressed wife, Colm made his way forward to the barricade, wondering how much further it was to the docks. In front of him, behind the opposite barricade, was a sea of British and Australian flags, and among them, standing in a small group of boys, was Dibs.

20 Colm tried to disappear into the crowd, but people were pushing him to the front. Colm saw Dibs turn towards the man standing behind him and say something. Then he turned and pointed towards Colm. Instinctively, he climbed over the barricade and ran up the street. A policeman
25 shouted at him, and someone in the crowd reached out for his arm, trying to drag him back behind the barricade, but Colm pulled free and kept running until he ran into a large chest in a blue uniform.

'Just what do you think you're doing, sonny?' asked the officer, gripping Colm's arms.

Colm looked around wildly. He didn't know where he was, he didn't know where to run to. He was ready to give up when he heard a growl and looked down to see Rusty pulling at the leg of the policeman's trousers.

'Get off, you bloody dog,' said the policeman, loosening his grip. Colm broke free. Rusty was close behind and then suddenly ahead of him. Colm followed the red fur through a mass of legs. Finally, Rusty turned into a side street and ran up the hill. Now, at last, Colm knew where he was and could find his way back to the asylum.

When Colm and Rusty finally pushed open the big doors of the asylum, an angry Bill was waiting for them.

After he had heard Colm's story, Bill sat down and put his head in his hands.

'Well you've messed things up good and proper,' he said. 'Everyone in Fremantle knows Rusty's my dog. If the coppers come knocking, we'll know why.'

Colm knelt down beside Rusty and put his arm around her. 'They won't take her away, will they? She was only trying to help me.'

'Right. Biting a copper. That's a big help. They'll probably take the pair of you away, lock you up and shoot her.'

Colm felt sick. 'Sorry,' he whispered.

Bill shook his head and sighed.

'No, it's not your fault. It's not right keeping you shut up in this place,' he said, as if talking to himself.

'Hanging around with the ghosts. But I can't let you loose in Fremantle, especially now. Sooner or later the police will come knocking on the door, and it will be back to Bindoon for you.'

'I'll run away again.'

'To what? It's not like the old days when there was always work about for boys. Little kid like you, you can't get a job or do anything much except wait to grow up.'

'I'll go back to England. Like you did, but the other way around.'

'Times have changed, mate. You'd never make it out of the port.'

Colm scowled. 'I have to get back to England. I have to get back to my mother. She's waiting for me.'

Bill leant forward and looked Colm straight in the eye.

'Listen, cobber, I know it's hard. But you've got to face it, mate. How long since you saw your ma? You reckon if she was alive, she'd give up on you? Do you know what happened to her?'

'She said she was coming back, but then…' Colm mumbled.

'Did she ever visit you? How long since you've seen her? Do you even remember her face?'

The questions were like punches to the stomach for Colm. He stood up and swept everything from the table. Tea and biscuits went flying to all corners of the room. He took hold of the edge of the table and gave it a push.

'I remember everything,' he shouted, and ran from the room.

In the old dining hall, he went to the piano and started beating out a song, while tears poured down his face.

'I can remember,' he muttered to himself as his fingers stumbled on the keys. He remembered that his mother played the violin. He remembered that she'd stand by the window while thin city sunlight shone through the glass and made her red hair shine. He could remember all sorts of little things about her – her favourite blue coat, the way she'd bring him a cake when she collected him from Mrs Fogarty's on Friday evening after her long day at work. But he couldn't remember her face. He could see everything, everything about her – the way she moved, the touch of her hand – but he couldn't make out her face. If he couldn't see her face, there could only be one reason.

12 The photograph

Next morning, Colm woke to find Bill packing pots and pans into a small wooden crate. Colm rubbed his eyes and looked around the room. It had always looked bare, but now there was almost nothing left of Bill's possessions.

5 Even Rusty's bowl was missing.

'Time to hit the frog and toad,' said Bill.

Colm felt as if he had been punched in the stomach. 'You're leaving home,' he said, more as a statement than a question.

10 The old man laughed. 'This old nut-house? A home? No, it was only a place to sleep for a season. Home is where the heart is and my heart feels easy on the open road. Been here too long already. Besides, after the trouble you caused yesterday, it's time we moved on. You up for an

15 adventure?'

Colm bent down and stroked Rusty. He didn't know how to answer. Why was Bill so kind to him, especially after last night? Rusty lowered her head and started licking Colm's feet.

20 'If Rusty wants me to come,' said Colm, 'I'll come.'

'She's not the one driving the ute,' said Bill, drily.

Colm bit his lip. 'Last night, I'm sorry for last night. It was 'cause … I've been waiting and thinking about … you know … for a long time … and when you said …'

25 'Never mind,' said Bill. 'You go and say your goodbyes to Ethel and the other ghosts. I've still got some packing up to do.'

All morning, Colm sat at the piano, playing every last tune he knew and then making up others. He wasn't sorry to be leaving the ghosts behind, but leaving the piano was like saying goodbye to an old friend.

'C'mon then,' said Bill, putting his head around the door. 'Tin Annie's waiting.'

5 'Who's she?'

Bill led Colm around to the side of the asylum. Parked out in the street was an old ute, rusty and scratched.

'Meet Tin Annie,' Bill announced. 'They used to call these old Fords Tin Lizzies. I've never fancied anyone
10 called Lizzie, but there was a girl in a blue dress that I liked when I was a young fella. Annie. She was always surprising, but a real goer. Old Tin Annie's like that too. Wouldn't call her reliable, but when she goes, she's a cracker of a car.'

Colm climbed into the front seat. Rusty jumped up
15 beside him and immediately sat on his lap.

'You're in her seat,' said Bill.

Colm smiled and wrapped his arms around her. 'It's our seat now.'

They drove out of Fremantle and onto the Great Eastern
20 Highway. The hills of Perth gave way to flat open country. Rusty kept climbing onto Colm's lap and sticking her head out the window, hanging her tongue out in the warm breeze. Colm put his hand into the wind and felt the air pass through his fingers.

25 As evening fell, Bill turned off the road onto a track and came to a stop.

'C'mon, mate. Time to catch some tucker.'

When Colm climbed out of Tin Annie he found Bill loading a rifle. In less than a minute, he'd scanned the
30 landscape and then fitted the gun to his shoulder. The first shot made Colm's insides hurt. It was as if it went straight through him. Twenty feet from where they stood, a rabbit

fell in the dirt. Bill turned and smiled. 'There you go. You nip over there and pick it up.'

The dead rabbit was warm in Colm's hands. He held the animal close against his chest.

5 'Give us that,' said Bill, frowning. 'You shouldn't carry it like that. You've got blood all over your shirt now. Haven't you ever been hunting?'

Colm shook his head.

Bill laid the rabbit down beside him and put a hand on 10 Colm's shoulder. 'Your turn. You take a shot at them. This time of night, they're everywhere. Easy to bring 'em down.'

Colm put his hands behind his back.

'C'mon. Every boy wants to have a go with a gun.'

15 'No, thank you,' said Colm.

'There's nothing to be afraid of. I'll show you how to shoot.'

Colm shook his head again and took a step away.

'Have it your way,' Bill said, raising the gun and firing 20 into the scrub. This time he sent Rusty to collect the rabbit.

Colm couldn't watch as Bill skinned the rabbits. He climbed back into Tin Annie and sat looking out at the landscape through the dusty windscreen. What was he doing out here? He lay down on the seat and shut his eyes, 25 wishing that when he opened them he'd be somewhere else, in a bed in a house, some place where he didn't have to feel so miserable and alone.

Bill opened the car door.

'Get out here and make yourself useful.'

30 While Colm gathered some more sticks for the fire, Bill cooked the rabbits in a billycan. They ate in silence. It was

as if both of them were suddenly wondering how they had come to be together.

After tea, Bill dragged two swags out of the back of the ute and unrolled them beside the camp fire.

5 'Aren't you going to put up a tent?' asked Colm.

'A tent? Why would we be wanting a tent?'

Colm didn't reply. He wished they were at least under a tree. The landscape seemed so wide, so vast, with no end to it. The night sky was full of stars. He whistled softly for

10 Rusty to come and lie beside him, but she was sleeping next to her master and didn't react. Colm stood up and tiptoed over to the old ute. He closed the windows and lay down on the old blanket that covered the seat.

Next morning, Colm woke to the smell of damper and

15 sweet tea. Bill laughed at him as he climbed out of the ute.

'Didn't want to sleep on the ground, eh? You frightened of snakes or something? A real Irishman.'

'Irishmen aren't afraid of snakes,' said Colm.

'There's no snakes in Ireland to be afraid of,' said Bill,

20 shaking his head and pouring tea from the billy into a tin cup. 'Saint Patrick drove them out, you should know that, if you're Irish, that is.'

Colm folded his arms across his chest. He wanted to say of course he was Irish, but he didn't really know if he had

25 been born in Ireland or England.

'You don't know about being Irish, either,' said Colm. Bill laughed. 'I know a bit. I was born there.'

He fed the rest of his damper to Rusty and stared out into the scrub, waiting for Bill to argue with him. But the

30 old man was in no hurry to say anything. He began rolling his cigarettes for the day. As he finished each one, he carefully put it into his tobacco tin.

'I was a couple of years older than you when my mam died. That was nearly sixty years ago.'

'Is that why you feel sorry for me? Because you were an orphan too? You don't have to help me. I'm not like you,' said Colm.

'No, I don't doubt that,' said Bill. He lit up one of his cigarettes.

'The thing is, when you help someone out, you don't know if something good is going to come of it, or if it's just your duty. But you have to do what you think is right. You have to help that stranger. Might be you're helping an angel, like happens in the Bible stories. Or that stranger might turn out to be your best mate.'

'I'm not an angel,' said Colm.

'Ain't that the truth. But when Rusty found you on the docks, well, I reckon she was trying to show me something. She's a wise old dog, that one. Perhaps we should pay attention to what she was trying to tell us.'

Bill got to his feet and kicked out the campfire.

'You don't have to sleep outside, you don't have to learn to shoot and you don't have to agree with me. But if we're going to be travelling companions for a while, you're gonna have to pull your weight and you're gonna have to leave me to my own way of seeing things. That's what mates do. What do you reckon?'

No one had ever asked Colm what he thought before. He'd always been told what he should think and how he should behave. For a moment he didn't know how to answer, but then Rusty licked his hands again.

'I think Rusty's wise too. So I suppose that means you and I should be mates.'

The next night, when they camped off the road, Colm put his blanket and pillow straight into the cab of the ute. He woke early in the grey light before dawn. Bill and Rusty were still asleep and breakfast would be a while yet.

5 He opened the glovebox. Inside were Bill's tobacco and a book of maps. Colm pulled out the map book and looked through it. When he found the map of Western Australia, he tried to find where they were. Just as he was about to put it back into the glovebox, a small square of card fell out
10 from between the pages. It was a black-and-white photograph of a woman, the same size as his holy card of the Blessed Virgin. The woman wore a pale coat and a small, elegant hat. She stood alone, smiling. His mother had worn a coat almost exactly like the one this woman
15 was wearing. He turned the picture over. On the back there were two words: 'Blue Delaney – 1949'. Colm said it softly to himself. It sounded like a flower.

Colm didn't know what his mother's name had been, but he liked the idea that it might have been 'Blue'. The
20 colour of the sky. And Delaney was a good Irish name, the sort of name she might have had before she married his father. Even though he knew this couldn't be a picture of her, it didn't hurt anyone if he pretended.

Colm knew he should put the picture back in the book
25 of maps, but instead, he put it into the battered old Bible that he'd taken from the asylum and said a prayer.

As the weeks turned into months, Colm started to see
what Bill had meant when he'd said the road was his
home. They never spent more than two nights camped at
the same stop, never more than three days on the same
5 job. Bill could turn his hand to anything, from carpentry to
horse-shoeing, lock-smithing, knife-sharpening or boot
repairs.

They travelled through the countryside, stopping at
small towns for supplies and driving out to isolated places
10 to see if there was any work. Colm would lie low, waiting
in the front seat of Tin Annie with Rusty while Bill looked
for work or shopped for supplies. Neither of them wanted
anyone asking too many questions about why Colm wasn't
in school. But when they were out in the open countryside,
15 Colm would help Bill with whatever task was at hand,
sorting through his tools and carrying materials. He
especially liked it when they would go door-knocking to
see who needed their knives or garden tools sharpened.
Bill had a grinding wheel and Colm loved to set the wheel
20 spinning while Bill sharpened the knives, the sparks flying
from the grindstone. If there was nothing else for him to
do, he'd sit under a tree with Rusty and read his Bible.

Colm celebrated his first Christmas away from Bindoon
in an open field, camped beneath a giant tree. Bill didn't
25 seem very interested in Christmas, and when Colm asked
if they could maybe go to mass on Christmas Day he said
that he'd rather pray in an open field.

On Christmas Eve they set up camp just like any other
night of the year, and just like any other night, when the

campfire grew low, Bill settled down in his swag and Colm climbed into the front seat of Tin Annie to sleep. But sleep wouldn't come to him, no matter how hard he tried. He sat up and looked out at the grass shining silvery white in the moonlight.

Colm opened the door of Tin Annie. Bill sat up.

'What's wrong, mate?' he asked.

'I can't sleep,' said Colm.

Bill ran his hand through his hair and sighed. 'C'mon over here. Let's stir up the fire then,' he said.

Colm knelt by the campfire and pushed at the coals with a stick.

'Is it this business about tomorrow being Christmas Day?'

'It should be special.'

'It is special. It's the day before the races out at Tangmalangaloo.'

'Don't make jokes, please,' said Colm.

Bill threw more wood on the fire and sparks danced in the air above the flames. 'Was Christmas special at the orphanage? Are you missing your little friends?'

'No,' said Colm. He couldn't even begin to tell Bill how terrible Christmas had been in the past. 'I always wanted my mum to come but she never did.'

'My first Christmas away from my mam, that was bad. But that's not a story for Christmas Eve. You want to think about something cheerful, that'll put you to sleep. When I was a boy at school in Ireland, our Christmas play was Good King Wenceslas – though of course, I wasn't the King in the play, I was the fool, and made everyone laugh. What we need is our own Christmas play.'

Bill got to his feet and walked around the fire, acting out the parts and telling the story of the king and his fool. Colm wrapped his arms around his knees and watched with attention. By the time the play was at an end the fire had burnt low again. Rusty had fallen asleep curled up beside Colm, and he was sorry to have to leave her for the car.

'That was the best play I've ever seen,' said Colm.

Colm woke on Christmas morning to the sound of kookaburras laughing in the trees. He took out the picture of Blue Delaney and whispered, 'Merry Christmas, Blue Delaney.'

It was only when he sat up that he saw the present. Wrapped in brown paper, it sat on top of the dashboard.

'Go on then,' said Bill, leaning in through the car window. 'Open it. Father Christmas didn't come all the way here for nothing.'

Colm grinned. Inside the brown paper, sparkling in the Christmas morning sunshine, lay a harmonica. Colm stroked the metal.

'Play us a note or two.'

Colm put it to his lips and blew a single note.

'Well, that's a start.'

That day Colm sat in the shade of the trees, blowing on the harmonica until his throat was sore and his lips stung. In the evening, Bill boiled up a tinned Christmas pudding in the billy and then cut it into three parts. Rusty ate her piece even faster than Colm and then curled up beside Bill, ready for the night.

'Do you think Rusty would like to sleep in Tin Annie, with me, just for a change?' asked Colm.

Bill shook his head. 'Sorry, Sonny Jim. Maybe when you get around to sleeping outside, she'll change her habit and sleep next to you. But she and me, we both have to stick with the stars. You've got your prayers, and we've got them to see us through the dark night.'

'Maybe next Christmas,' said Colm.

'Maybe,' said Bill.

14   Nugget on the goldfields

Pingelly, Katanning, Kojonup, Gnowangerup; so many of
the towns they visited had strange-sounding names and
some of them Colm couldn't even pronounce. It didn't
seem to matter where they were, the rhythm of their days
5 was the same. Until they came to Kalgoorlie.

Kalgoorlie was quiet when Tin Annie drove into town.
Everything felt too bright and wide and the sun beat down
on them as hot as ever. Colm knelt on the seat and hung
out the window. It was so long since they'd been in a town
10 that everything looked exciting even though there weren't
many people around.

Bill pointed at a signpost that read 'Hannan Street'.

'You know, it was an Irishman that made this town.
First discovered gold here. They named this street after
15 him. Paddy Hannan, that was his name. Speaking of mad
Irishmen, there's an old mate of mine here in Kalgoorlie
that we should visit.'

They drove on in silence until they came to a turning in
the road.

20 'Here we go, that's where Nugget Malloy was last time I
came through this way. His wife Doreen, she loves kids,
her own kids, grandkids, all sorts of little kids. Always has
a lot of them around the place. Be good for you to be with
a bunch of young 'uns again.'

25 Colm didn't want to be with a bunch of kids. He'd got
used to being with just Bill and Rusty. He hugged Rusty
closer to him and watched the red dust as they turned onto
a dirt track. It didn't look as though there were any houses
out along this lonely road.

A bunch of kids ran out in front of the car as Bill brought it to a stop outside a battered tin shack. They had skin the colour of milky coffee and dark brown eyes. As soon as Bill and Colm climbed out of the ute, the kids climbed all over it, jumping in behind the wheel and laughing, tooting the old horn and climbing into the back. At the sound of the horn, a man stepped out of the shack and into the midday sun.

'Well, strike me lucky, Billy Dare!'

Nugget Malloy was a short man with a weathered face. Around his eyes there were deep smile lines. He wore a battered, dusty hat, and a dirty white shirt. He grinned at Bill.

Colm stood awkwardly behind Bill, one leg either side of Rusty, trying to keep her near him. But there was a crowd of dogs sniffing around Tin Annie and Rusty soon went to join them.

'See you've still got old Rusty with you, but who's the kid?' asked Nugget, looking Colm up and down.

Bill laughed but he seemed a little embarrassed. Colm looked down at the red dirt and drew a line in the dust with his toe. He wished they hadn't come here.

A plump, dark-skinned woman came out of the shack and joined in the talk.

Colm felt even shyer. He'd seen plenty of Aboriginal people in the towns they'd driven through but he'd never spoken with any of them. He hadn't thought, when Bill had mentioned Nugget's wife, that she would be anything other than white.

She kept glancing at Colm and smiling. Colm didn't know where to look. Bill pulled out some rabbits from the back of the ute and handed them to Doreen.

'Thanks, Bill. You never come empty-handed,' said Doreen. She handed the rabbits to one of the children and then reached out and patted Colm's hair. 'This one's nearly the same age as our Rosie.'

5 'That's right,' said Nugget. 'Rosie can sort the boy. You and me can do our catching up down the pub, old mate.' He put his arm through Bill's and drew him over to the ute.

'I've been on the wagon for a while now,' said Bill, 10 sounding uneasy.

'Billy Dare on the wagon? C'mon, mate,' said Nugget, pulling open Tin Annie's door and climbing inside. 'We'll be home late, Dor,' he called.

Colm folded his arms across his chest and glared at 15 them. What was he meant to do now? As if Bill knew what he was thinking, he turned and winked. 'I'll be back, Sonny Jim. You keep an eye on Rusty.'

Colm called Rusty over to him. Doreen yelled out to someone in the bungalow in a language that Colm didn't 20 understand. The door banged open and a tall, slim girl around eleven years old came out with a plump baby boy on her arm.

'I'm Rosie,' she said, looking at Colm. 'Mum says I've gotta keep an eye on you.'

25 'Why doesn't she speak English?' asked Colm. 'I didn't understand what she was saying.'

'She only speaks English when Dad's around. Dad doesn't like it when she speaks our language, but she reckons we'll never learn it if she don't speak it,' said 30 Rosie.

The bungalow looked untidy with its battered verandah, but inside it was comfortable. In one corner was a big bed with a coloured blanket thrown across it, and in the middle of the room stood a table with a golden-brown loaf of hot and steaming damper and an open tin of dark raspberry jam beside it.

Rosie went out onto the verandah and got a bottle of milk and a dish with butter on it. The smaller kids waited at the table, stretching out their hands as Doreen cut thick slices of damper and covered them with butter and jam. Colm stood in a corner of the room, wishing Bill would come back soon. He suddenly realised that Doreen had been speaking to him but he had been so wrapped up in his own thoughts that he hadn't heard her. She smiled at him, waiting for a reply.

'You not hungry?' said Rosie loudly, as if she were talking to an idiot. 'Mum makes real good damper. You gotta try it.'

Colm couldn't remember the last time he had tasted jam. Rosie smiled at him from across the table. 'You old Bill's grandkid, are ya?' she asked.

Colm shrugged uncertainly, damper halfway to his mouth, 'Are you Nugget's granddaughter?'

Rosie laughed. 'Nah, he's my dad.'

Colm looked at the crowd of faces around the table.

'Are all these kids your brothers and sisters?'

Rosie rolled her eyes. 'Nah, these are my big sister's kids and some of them are cousins and … well, they're all our mob anyway.'

Colm wondered if he had cousins, somewhere in the world. If he did, maybe there was an auntie like Doreen who would invite him for afternoon tea.

Doreen spoke to Rosie again in that strange language that Colm couldn't understand. Rosie answered her in English and then looked at Colm.

'C'mon, you, I'll show you around.'

Colm followed Rosie out into the dry scrub. She led him down a track and stopped to break something from a tree. Colm was surprised when she put it straight into her mouth.

'Here, you, help me get up and I'll get you some too.' She climbed onto Colm's back before he even had time to answer and tore from a branch a handful of some strange plant with small buds on it.

'Good tucker this. I think your mob call it mistletoe, but round here they call it *tjitjiku mai* – good for kids.'

Not as sweet as jam, but good lollies, and they're free. Try it.'

Colm put some of the plant into his mouth. She was right. It was sweet and it made his mouth feel and fresh. He thought of how hungry he'd been on the long walk from Bindoon, yet he'd walked straight past trees that had this sort of mistletoe hanging on them.

They kept walking and all the while Rosie chatted, telling him everything about her family, about her dad and her big sister who worked on a station somewhere outside Kalgoorlie. There were so many people in Rosie's family that Colm had trouble keeping track of them all. After a while, he stopped listening. He wondered when he'd hear the sound of Tin Annie coming up the dirt track.

Rosie showed him the shaft that Nugget was mining. He was a prospector, trying to scrape a living from the small amount of gold it produced.

As the afternoon wore on and Bill didn't return, Colm began to grow uneasy. He couldn't eat any of the food Doreen had prepared for tea. He sat with Rusty just outside the front door, waiting for Bill.

5 Colm woke at dawn. Doreen had covered him up with a blanket and Rusty was close, warm against his chest. All morning, he paced backwards and forwards outside the bungalow, staring down the track that led to Kalgoorlie. Rosie grew tired of trying to talk to him and wandered off
10 into the bush with one of the younger children. By midday, Colm couldn't stand it any longer. Whistling Rusty to him, he set off down the track.

The shadows were long, stretching all the way across the wide streets of Kalgoorlie when Colm walked into
15 town. He saw Tin Annie straight away, parked outside a corner hotel. All his worry disappeared at the sight of it. But when he stopped and looked into the car, there was no one in it. He walked over to the pub and stared in through the windows. There were men at the bar but none
20 of them looked like Bill or Nugget. He was standing next to Tin Annie wondering what to do next when he heard someone groaning. The sound came from the back of the ute. He stood on tiptoes and pulled himself high enough to look in. There, stretched out on his back, was Bill. Beside
25 him lay Nugget, his face red, his mouth open. Bill opened one bright blue eye and looked at Colm for a minute before he shut it again.

'Don't look at me like that, Sonny Jim,' said Bill.

'You're drunk,' said Colm.

30 'We had to celebrate. That's what you do, when you haven't seen an old mate in years. You celebrate.'

Nugget rolled over and turned his back to both of them.

'Doreen's been worried about you,' said Colm. It wasn't really true. Doreen had actually told Colm not to worry and that the two old men would be back.

'Well, we'll be back tonight. Couldn't bring Nugget home to Doreen until we'd both dried out, could I?'

Colm snorted. He wanted to shout at Bill. Didn't he understand that he couldn't just disappear? Didn't he realise that Colm had been sick with worry?

'C'mon, Rusty,' said Colm, turning to walk away. But the old dog jumped into the back of the ute. Colm heard Bill and Nugget groan. He sat down and buried his face in his hands.

When Bill announced they were staying at Nugget's for the week, Colm felt uneasy.

At first, Colm tried to keep to himself. He put his swag on the verandah so that he could watch for Bill and Nugget. He would take out his harmonica and play long tunes to make the hours pass more quickly.

Doreen and the other children would sit by a campfire a short distance away from the bungalow, and sometimes visitors from other nearby camps would come and join them. Rosie tried to get Colm to join the others but he stayed on the verandah.

'You know,' she said one evening, 'I reckon you're boring.' Then she got up and walked away.

Colm watched her disappear around the side of the bungalow and was suddenly ashamed. Every evening Rosie had stayed with him, missing the fun, and he'd never talked to her. For a while, he sat listening to the sounds of laughter and conversation. Finally he got to his feet and, whistling for Rusty to follow, he went round the back to join the others.

Rosie was sitting close to Doreen, listening. One of the little girls was in Doreen's lap and the other children leant against her as well. Colm stood on the edge of the firelight.

'Good to see you, Colm. You come sit with us,' said Doreen. 'About time you stopped worrying about that old man. This story, this one's for Rosie but maybe it's good for you too.

'The home of our people, Ngarrindjeri people, it's a long way from here at a place called Raukkan, way over in

South Australia. Raukkan, it means "the ancient way" and I'm gonna tell you about those ancient ways, the dreamings of our people. This story, it's as old as the night sky.'

Doreen's voice grew deep and sure as she began her
5 story. In the smoky night air, the words seemed like magic.

'See them stars? They're the *Mungingee*,' said Doreen, pointing at a bright cluster of stars in the sky. 'Those stars, they're our ancestors, wise girls, those stars.

'This is the story of those girls, those girls that became
10 the stars. Rosie, she's still just a little one. But one day, she'll be *Yartooka* like those girls up there. Long time ago, these girls, the *Yartooka*, they go to the Elders and they say, teach us. Teach us to fight hunger and pain and fear. So the Elders taught them. They begin to train them.

15 'Three years the girls learn with the Elders and then the Elders say, now is the time for the tests. For three days those girls have nothing to eat and travel long distance. Three days and no food, but they walk many, many miles through hard country. Then on the fourth day, they're
20 offered kangaroo meat for their tucker, but these girls only take a small piece. They know to be greedy makes them weak and to control their hunger makes them strong.

'Then they learn to fight pain. The Elders break their tooth, cut them until the blood runs and then rub ash into
25 the wounds but the girls, they know how to be strong, they fight that pain. And the Elders say, you want to do more tests? And the girls say yes, they will do what must be done. So that night, the Elders take the girls to a camp, and when the night comes the girls throw down their
30 blankets to sleep, but as they lie still something crawls over them and bites them all over. And then they see they are camped on ant-hills and the Elders are testing them. They

73

lie all night on the ant-hills but they don't complain. They fight the pain. And then in the morning, the Elders see these girls have fought pain and won.

'Then the Elders say there is one more thing that they must learn, one more thing they must conquer, and that is fear. That night, they tell stories of the spirits, the ghosts that will come, bad spirits that will steal them away. The shadows start to move, and the girls, they grow afraid, and then the Elders tell them this is the burial place of their great-grandfathers. And the girls lie in that burial place all night and they fight the fear and in the morning, the Elders see the girls have stayed at the burial place and fought their fears and won.

'And the Elders and all the people celebrate these girls, these brave and strong *Yartooka*. The Great Spirit, he was so happy with these girls he sent the Star Spirit to them and the Star Spirit gathers up the seven sisters and takes them up to the sky. No more suffering for those girls. They shine a light for everyone, for everyone who is afraid. When you feel hunger or pain or fear, especially if you're afraid, you look to the sisters. The sisters, they help you do any brave thing that must be done.'

Colm looked up. Rosie leant closer to him and took his hand, using it to point out the stars Doreen was talking about. The Seven Sisters shone out in a bright cluster.

Jimmy, the littlest of Doreen's grandkids, came and sat down on Colm's lap. His skin felt warm and silky. Colm sat very still. He didn't want to frighten the little boy. When the fire grew low and Jimmy had fallen asleep, Colm carried him back to the bungalow and laid him in the big old bed.

Every evening from then on, Colm joined the other children around the campfire while Doreen told stories. Sometimes they were about her family and things that had happened to them. Sometimes they were like fairy-tales, stories from another time and place where animals talked and people had magic inside them. In Doreen's stories everything had a spirit, even rain and sunshine, and every spirit had a story.

Somehow, all the stories connected up, like a great big pattern that everyone and everything was a part of.

Every night Colm stopped for a moment and looked up at the Seven Sisters shining brightly above them. Bill had told him that they were also called the Pleiades and that sailors used the stars to guide their journeys across the ocean, but Colm liked to think of them as seven girls like Rosie. If he could have a sister, he would have wanted her to be just like Rosie. Sisters, brothers, aunties, uncles and cousins were like parts of a whole family that he'd never thought about before now. At least Colm had Bill and Rusty – but did that count?

16 Stolen

Colm was showing all the boys how to make Rusty fetch things when the big black car bumped down the road towards the bungalow in a cloud of dust. Doreen saw it first and instantly called for Rosie.

5 'Rosie! Boys, come quick!' There was fear in her voice that made both Colm and Jimmy start to run.

She gave the baby, Barbara, to Rosie and then pushed Jimmy to Colm. 'You take 'em out back. Hide until I call you. You don't come sooner, understand?' she said. Then

10 she hurried the other two boys inside and shut the door.

'C'mon,' called Rosie, running up the hill behind the bungalow. Colm followed, feeling his fear grow.

At the top, they both turned to look back. A policeman was arguing with Doreen while another was trying to

15 catch Barry and Ted, the two little boys Doreen had tried to hide in the bungalow. Colm saw the officer finally catch them and push them into the big black car while Doreen was held, struggling and shouting, by the other officers. Another policeman was running up the hill, heading

20 straight for Colm and Rosie.

'Run, run,' shouted Rosie, grabbing Colm by the wrist and pulling him away. 'Don't let them catch you!'

'Let go,' said Colm. 'I can run faster if you let go.'

As soon as he was free, Colm sprinted forward, holding

25 Jimmy close to his chest. He could feel Rosie behind him. His heart beat loudly in his ears. Jimmy started to cry because Colm was holding him so tightly. Colm could see Rosie was having trouble holding Barbara.

They both ran for some rocks where they could hide, putting down the two small children. Barbara and Jimmy looked frightened, their dark eyes wide. Rosie put her finger to her lips. 'No crying,' she said. She looked out
5 from between two rocks.

'What's going on?' asked Colm in a whisper.

'They're gonna try and take us away. Some of Mum's first kids, they got taken before I was born. I've got a big brother called Pat and I've never even seen him. Emily,
10 these ones' mum, she got taken away too, but she was bigger and she came back. When I was little, Mum used to dig a hole and cover me up in it. I used to have to sit quiet as a mouse. But they don't mess with us when Dad's home. I wish Dad was here.'

15 'That's crazy,' said Colm. 'You're a family. They don't take kids away from families.' He suddenly felt fear as he said it. Maybe it was really him they were after, not Rosie and the others. Maybe they knew he wasn't anyone's boy, that he didn't belong to any of the grown-ups, and they
20 had come to take him back to Bindoon.

'Bloody hell,' said Rosie . 'He's coming this way. We're gonna have to run for it again.

'We'll separate,' she said. 'He can only follow one of us.'

Before Colm could reply, she'd run out from behind the
25 rock and was zig-zagging down the hillside. Colm picked up Jimmy and started to run. When he heard the policeman's footsteps behind him, it gave wings to his feet. He had to run faster than the man. Holding Jimmy so tight that the little boy cried out, he ran as hard and as fast as he
30 could.

When he stopped, neither Rosie nor the policeman was anywhere in sight. He felt as if he had run for miles. His arms ached and Jimmy was crying. Colm put the little boy down and scanned the horizon for a sign of Rosie.

'Want Nani!' Jimmy cried. Colm picked him up and started back towards bungalow. He tried to make Jimmy be quiet, in case the police were still there, but when he looked over the top of the hill, the black car was nowhere in sight.

Doreen was sitting alone in the dust, bent over like an old woman. For a moment, Colm thought someone had beaten her, she looked so crumpled and broken. Her face and clothes were covered in dust and her eyes were red from crying.

She stared at Colm for a moment as if she didn't know him and then she reached her arms out for Jimmy. Jimmy started crying again as Colm handed him back, and she held him close against her body, rocking the small boy back and forth and sobbing along with him. Colm had never seen an adult cry. It made him want to run away again, to run as far from her unhappiness as he could. But he knew Doreen needed him.

He went into the bungalow and set the kettle to boil. When the water was ready, he made a pot of strong black tea. He put four spoonfuls of sugar in a cup and poured the hot water over it. His hands were trembling.

Doreen was still weeping and rocking Jimmy in her arms. He knelt down beside her in the dust and offered her the tea.

'They took Rosie and Barbara, didn't they?' he asked.

Doreen simply nodded and shut her eyes. Colm didn't know what to say. He stared at his bare feet. His eyes felt hot and he rubbed them with the back of his hand. Then a single tear dripped onto his leg, and then another. Doreen slipped an arm around him and drew him closer to her. Jimmy reached out and touched Colm's face. The three of them sat together in the dust and cried.

Later, when it was almost dark and there were no more tears left to cry, they went back into the bungalow and Doreen lit a lamp. Jimmy fell asleep in Doreen's arms as she sat silently waiting. When they heard Tin Annie pull into the yard, Colm ran outside to Bill. He'd spent the afternoon feeling angry with the old men, but at the sight of them he burst into tears.

Nugget came into the bungalow and realised what had happened. He picked up the sugar bowl from the table and threw it against a wall. Doreen held Jimmy close.

'What the hell were you doing, you stupid cow!' Nugget yelled at Doreen. He turned and kicked the wall then marched across the room towards Doreen.

Colm leapt between them.

'It's not her fault!' he shouted. 'Where were you? Why weren't you here, looking after them?'

Nugget's face turned even redder and he clenched his fists, but before anyone could speak another word, Bill grabbed Colm by the arm and dragged him outside. They could hear the sound of things flying around the bungalow and then Nugget shouting again. This time, Doreen shouted back. Bill marched Colm over to Tin Annie and opened the door.

'Get in.'

'No,' shouted Colm, trying to break free of Bill's grip.

'It's not fair.'

'Doreen can sort him without you making things worse. That's just Nugget. It's his way.'

'It's a stupid way! Why doesn't he do something? Why don't you do something?'

Colm clenched his fists. What was the point of being a grown-up if you were as helpless as a child?

'You wait here,' said Bill, pushing Colm into the front seat of Tin Annie and then turning back to the bungalow.

Colm could hear Bill's voice beneath the roar of Nugget's anger.

When everything was quiet again, Colm climbed out of the ute and tiptoed over to the bungalow. The adults were talking in normal voices now. He opened the door and saw Nugget sitting at the table with a cup of tea in front of him. Doreen was beside him, one hand on Nugget's shoulder. Colm couldn't believe she'd forgiven him so quickly. He came into the room and stood behind Bill.

'So what are you going to do?' asked Colm. Nugget shrugged.

'They've probably sent 'em to Moore River. It's where they took Pat, Doreen's other boy.'

'Then you have to go and get them back,' said Colm.

'Jesus, mate,' said Nugget, looking to Bill. 'Can you get that kid to shut up?'

'He doesn't usually have this much to say,' said Bill.

'They probably won't give me Emily's kids, but I might get Rosie. I'll have to go to Perth to try. I don't know. Me and Doreen, we're not married – couldn't get permission, so I just took her out of the state.'

'Do you want me to come?' asked Bill.

It was Doreen who decided. She looked around the whole table, her dark eyes resting for a moment on each face.

'No, Nugget goes alone,' she said. 'I have to go home, and Bill, you have to take care of this boy of yours. That's how it has to be.'

Bill opened his mouth to argue but Nugget lifted a hand to silence him.

'Dor's right. Crikey, Bill, I taught you how to fight, didn't I? I can fight my own battles. I'll get the girl back, one way or another.'

'If there's anything we can do,' said Bill uncertainly.

'I don't want to leave her and the little one alone. The welfare have been watching us for a long time now, and they'll be back. Reckon you could drive Dor and the little one to Ceduna and put 'em on the train there?'

'This isn't my country,' explained Doreen. 'My people, the Ngarrindjeri, they're from Raukkan. White fellas call it Point McLeay, near where the Murray River meets the sea. I can maybe keep Jimmy safe with me there.'

'Are you sure about this?' asked Bill, looking from Doreen to Nugget. 'If you want me to help you out in Perth …'

'You got your own worries, Bill,' said Nugget, shaking his head. 'You'll lose that kid of yours if you're not careful and I know how much he means to you.'

Colm was astonished. Bill had hardly spoken to him since they'd arrived in Kalgoorlie. Colm had started to think Bill had even forgotten his real name as he hadn't called him anything but 'Sonny Jim' for weeks.

That evening everyone went to bed early, exhausted by the terrible events of the afternoon. Bill brought his swag out onto the verandah, alongside Colm's, and they lay talking in the darkness.

'Thank God they didn't get you, too,' said Bill.

'But why did they take the others?' asked Colm. 'I don't understand. I thought it was me they were after.'

'The thing is, the authorities reckon it ain't right for a black woman to raise a white man's kids,' said Bill. 'The black fellas … they're not like citizens in the way white people are.'

'That's stupid! Why not?'

'Well, that's a good question,' said Bill. He sounded uncomfortable. He didn't seem to have good answers to any of Colm's questions.

Colm lay on his side, puzzling out what had happened. Every way he turned it, it was wrong. People did such stupid, terrible things to each other. It made him glad that he believed in God. At least God didn't do stupid things. He put his hands together and began to pray.

'What are you whispering there?' asked Bill.

'I'm praying,' said Colm.

Bill turned his back on Colm. 'Waste of breath, if you ask me. Prayers won't change the law.'

'I'm praying to Our Lady so she'll watch over the children until they get back to Doreen.'

Bill didn't reply. Colm added an extra prayer for Billy Dare.

The next morning, Doreen packed her and Jimmy's things into a battered suitcase and put it in the back of Tin Annie. Colm and Rusty jumped into the back as well so that Doreen and Jimmy could share the front seat.

When all the goodbyes had been said, Bill fixed a tarp over the top of Colm and Rusty so that the sun wouldn't burn them.

'There you go, Sonny Jim,' said Bill. 'You ready for the open road again?'

'Yes, but can I ask a favour?'

'You can ask,' said Bill.

5 'Please don't call me "Sonny Jim" any more. I have a name, my own name. You never use my real name. You always call me other things. My name is Colm.'

Bill laughed.

'All right, Colm it is, then. But if you and I are going to
10 stay together, I reckon one of us should be changing their name. See, all this trouble, it's given me a lot to think about. I reckon if people think you've run away, someone might take you away.'

'What do you mean?'

15 Bill put his hands on Colm's shoulders and looked him in the face. 'I reckon you ought to call me Grandad from now on. That way no one is going to go asking us questions, eh? I don't have any grandkids of my own, but if I did that's what I'd want them to call me – Grandad.'

20 Colm smiled. It felt strange to be so happy after all the tears of the day before, to feel the warmth of it fill him up like sweet tea.

'All right, Grandad,' he said.

17 The Dog Fence

....

There was plenty of time to think in the long drive across the Nullarbor. Sometimes Colm could hear Doreen crying over the noise of the engine. Rusty flattened her ears at the sound. She didn't like it any more than Colm. When
5 Jimmy shouted 'Nani, Nani', over and over again, Doreen's voice became a hum of comforting sounds. Colm pulled out his harmonica and played the happiest tunes he could think of in the hope it would cheer everyone up.

Colm found himself practising the word 'Grandad' over
10 and over again. When they stopped to camp overnight and Bill handed him a plate of beans for his dinner, Colm said, 'Thanks, Grandad!' so loudly that both Bill and Doreen laughed, for the first time since leaving Kalgoorlie.

At the train station in Ceduna, Doreen took Colm's face
15 in her hands and kissed him on the forehead. Colm shut his eyes and took in the warmth of her skin, the scent of her hands.

'You take care of that old fella,' she whispered. 'And if you get worried out there in that desert, you look up at the
20 Seven Sisters and let them light your darkness, eh? And we both say our prayers and maybe Rosie'll find her way home again soon.'

The train pulled out of the station and Jimmy stood on Doreen's lap and pressed his face against the glass, waving
25 at Colm. Colm waved back.

'It was a good thing you saved Jimmy,' said Bill. 'I reckon Doreen's heart would have broken without a little one to take care of.'

'But I didn't save Rosie,' said Colm.

'A man can only do his best and your best was bloody good,' said Bill.

As they drove out of Ceduna, Bill said, 'I've heard from an old mate that there's work going on the Dog Fence. Thought I might take it.'

The Victoria Desert began to stretch out in front of them as they left town. They drove north towards the Dog Fence, through a wide, open landscape of earth and sky.

It was slow and hot travelling along the Dog Fence. The more they drove inland, the hotter the air became until Colm felt he was breathing fire. It was like being in a furnace. He and Rusty tried sticking their heads out the window, but it was worse than the burning heat inside the car. The sandy air hurt Colm's skin and made his eyes sore. He pulled his head back inside. There was nothing to see except scrub and tough little grasses in the rock and sand, and the fence stretching like a thin grey scar across the landscape.

'What if we break down?' asked Colm.

'Don't you worry about that. They used to do the fence on camel, but these days they use jeeps. Tin Annie here, she's part camel with a bit of jeep thrown in, so she'll be fine.'

'But what if we get lost?'

Bill smiled. 'We'll follow the fence, mate. It's more than three thousand miles long and there's no way we can lose it.'

Bill stopped next to the fence where an emu had crashed into it. They both climbed out of the ute.

Bill shook his head. 'She's hit the fence very fast, this one. Seems she broke her neck.'

In the distance, another emu was running across the desert. 'See, they get faster and faster. They can go 30 miles an hour but they don't see the fence until they've hit it.'

Colm helped Bill as he looked for the tools he would need for the job and then climbed back into Tin Annie to wait while Bill repaired the fence. Later they stopped to fill in a hole made by a wombat. The day dragged on. They drove so slowly that Colm got tired looking at the fence. When he shut his eyes, he saw the endless fence moving along in his head. Despite the flies and the heat, he fell asleep. When he woke up, it was to the sound of Bill repairing a fencepost.

Colm's shirt was wet with sweat. He went round to the back of the ute and drank from the billycan. The water was as warm as tea, but it was good to wet his throat. Flies buzzed around his face and although he tried hard to swat them away, they came back. Colm felt as if he was inside a strange and terrifying dream.

The days dragged on, long and boring. Colm's neck was sore from always turning his head one way to watch the fence. After a few days, he started to fill the wombat holes while Bill repaired the holes in the fence. They filled up the billycans at every dam or tank, and ate tinned beef and tinned vegetables until Colm felt he couldn't take another mouthful of them. The nearest town was hundreds of miles away

One morning, Rusty wasn't in camp when they rose. Colm helped Bill pack up the breakfast dishes, and all the while he scanned the scrub, looking for a sign of movement.

'Where is that dog?' said Bill. He put two fingers into his mouth and whistled. Nothing moved.

'I'll find her,' said Colm. He walked into the scrub. If he closed his eyes and willed it, then he should be able to feel Rusty wherever she was. He was sure she was quite close.

When he opened his eyes, saw something move in the dust. Rusty was under a bush: she was shaking violently.

'Bill,' called Colm, 'Bill, here, I've found her! But something's wrong! Hurry!'

Bill knelt beside the dog. When he touched her body, Rusty shook even more violently.

'What is it?' asked Colm.

'Snakebite, maybe, maybe not.'

Rusty started shaking as if there was electricity running through her. Colm was cold with fear.

'What's wrong?' he cried, feeling tears in his eyes.

'I think she's taken dingo bait. Poison. It might be better for her if we killed her.'

Colm walked beside Bill as he carried Rusty over to the ute and put her on her blanket in the back. He picked up the knife he used to kill rabbits.

'No! What are you doing!' Colm grabbed Bill's hand. 'We have to save her.'

'Get out of my way,' said Bill. He pushed Colm away and held Rusty's head. Quickly, he made cuts on the side of Rusty's ears. Blood poured down.

'Now go and fill the billycan.' Bill pushed it at Colm, and then looked for something in the food bag.

When Colm returned, Bill threw lots of salt into the water.

Bill took Rusty in his arms.

'Now I'll keep her mouth open. I want you to pour the salty water straight down her throat.'

The salt water made Rusty throw up. When Bill put her down she staggered around the ute, vomiting again and again. As soon as they could, they poured more salt water down her throat. Finally, when she'd finished, Bill put her
5 on her old blanket in the shade. Bill and Colm knelt beside her and massaged her. 'Here, you need a break,' said Bill. 'Go get yourself a drink and sit in the car. I'll call you if I need you.'

'What are you going to do? You can't shoot her, Bill.
10 You can't.'

'I'm hoping it won't come to that.' Colm walked back to Tin Annie, holding back tears.

The morning got hotter. For a while, Colm fell asleep and then, when he woke, felt ashamed. He took the photo
15 of Blue Delaney out of the glovebox and prayed as hard as he could. He was still praying when he heard Rusty bark – a thin, hollow sort of bark, but a bark. He ran across to where she lay with her head resting in Bill's lap.

'I prayed for her,' said Colm. 'Maybe it helped.'
20 'Maybe it did,' said Bill. 'Between your prayers and my hard work, she'll be back to her old self in no time.'

That night, Colm stayed by the fire with Rusty nuzzled up against him. He didn't want to get back into Tin Annie to sleep. When Bill's steady breathing changed to snores,
25 Colm pulled out the photo from his pocket and held it towards the flame. He liked seeing the bright face by firelight.

'Thanks, Blue,' he whispered. He was sure his prayers had helped save Rusty. He looked up at the Seven Sisters
30 and felt that someone, somewhere, was looking out for all of them.

18   The letter

By the time they reached the border of the Northern
Territory, every bone in Colm's body was aching. Even
when he lay down at night, he could feel the bump of each
corrugation they had driven over. In his mind, he could
5 see those endless red ridges – thousands and thousands of
them – that Tin Annie had chugged across in the journey
north.

Every evening they'd drive over to the side of the road
and camp. Colm had got used to sleeping out under the
10 stars now, even though the nights were cold. He felt it was
growing inside him, this love of the desert.

The days grew into a rhythm of dust and driving. They
could drive for hours without seeing another living soul
and then suddenly, like a mirage, a herd of camels would
15 appear. Other times a cloud would signal the arrival of
another car, though it was a long time before the vehicle
actually came into view.

Bill always knew where to find water, as if he had a
map of the desert. Often it was salty and Colm would still
20 be thirsty after drinking it, sometimes it was so sweet and
clean it would make his whole body thankful for its
freshness.

On a hot Saturday afternoon, a line of hills appeared on
the horizon.

25 'Alice Springs coming up,' said Bill pointing ahead.

'In those hills?' asked Colm.

'No, we pass through Heavitree Gap to get there. Those
are the MacDonnell Ranges, oldest mountains in the
world.'

As they drove through the gap, Tin Annie started to make loud banging noises. It was as if she knew they were coming near to a place where she could rest. Colm hung out the window and looked up at the high MacDonnell Ranges. After months in flat country, it was strange to look upwards and see something other than sky.

They crossed a dry riverbed and the town appeared ahead. Colm felt excitement in his chest. This was a proper town, the first they'd seen since leaving Ceduna. There were wide streets and trees and green lawns. People walking along the footpaths turned to stare at the loud explosions Tin Annie made as she chugged to a stop outside the Alice Springs Hotel.

Colm felt ten pounds lighter when he stepped out of the shower. The water had taken the desert away. Laid out on the bed in their hotel room Bill had left a new shirt and a pair of shorts for him. The clothing felt like silk against his clean skin.

Colm had never eaten in a restaurant in his life. Sitting at a proper table in the hotel dining room was like eating in a palace. They both ordered steak and vegetables and Colm had a lemon soda and then jelly and ice cream. After the months of salt beef and tinned vegetables or rabbit and kangaroo meat, it seemed impossible that anything could taste so delicious.

'Good to see you back in the Alice, Billy Dare.' A short man marched across the dining room and pulled up a chair at their table.

'Colm, this is Ted Kelly,' said Bill uneasily. 'He runs this establishment.'

'I thought maybe the young man was part of your show,' said Mr Kelly. 'Looks a lot like your Clancy. Is he Clancy's boy, your grandson maybe?'

'Not Clancy's boy,' said Bill, 'but yeah, he is my grandson. We're just passing through, Ted. I've been out of the business for a long time now. Too old for that.'

'That's a shame, mate,' Ted said, shaking his head. He turned to Colm. 'Your grandad was one of the best actors in the business. He was a bloody legend.'

Bill ordered another beer. 'Look, Ted, that was a long time ago, mate. No one wants to see that old melodrama any more.'

'Showing me age, am I?' said Ted. 'Well, I'm glad you arrived safely. We were starting to worry you'd never get here.'

'Someone on the track tell you I was coming?'

'No, I've got mail for you. From Melbourne. Been waiting here for you a couple of months.' Ted told one of the waiters to go and fetch the letter from his office. 'I was going to return it to the sender but they wrote "Hold" on the envelope so I guess they was hoping you'd pass through here eventually. Return address was for some girl called Blue Delaney in Williamstown. She a relation?' asked Ted.

Bill ran one hand through his silvery hair. He leant across the table towards Colm. 'Cobber, why don't you go and order yourself another bowl of ice cream. Ask Larry up there at the bar. He'll see to it.'

The last thing Colm wanted to do was leave the table just when the conversation was getting interesting. 'But I don't want any more ice cream, Grandad. I'm full—'

'Even if you don't want a treat, Rusty is ready for one. Here, Ted, do you reckon the cook could give the boy a bone for the dog? She's waiting in the ute.' It was cold outside so Colm took an extra blanket out of the back and
5 folded it around Rusty. It would be the first night in months they hadn't slept together. He wished he could take her up into their hotel room, but he didn't want to risk annoying Bill. The mention of Blue Delaney always changed his mood, and not for the better.

10 Colm woke in the middle of the night, startled to find himself surrounded by walls. He wasn't the only one who couldn't sleep. Standing on the balcony was Bill, his cigarette glowing red in the darkness.

Next morning, when Colm came down into the foyer of
15 the hotel he found Bill sitting in the courtyard with a beer in front of him. It was like a warning signal. He was reading a letter. Colm sat on the seat opposite. Bill looked up at Colm crumpling the pages of the letter in his hand.

'What's wrong, Grandad?' asked Colm, feeling his heart
20 beat faster. There were so many questions he wanted to ask.

'When you've finished your brekky, get upstairs and put your things together,' Bill said. 'We're leaving town this morning.'

25 'But we only just got here. You said we were going to stay here a while.'

'Well, I changed my mind.'

'Was it the letter? Are we going to see Blue Delaney?' Bill took another mouthful of beer, emptying the glass,
30 and then signalled for the waiter to bring him another.

'No,' he said, bitterly. 'No hope of that. But it set me thinking about things.'

Colm kept staring at him, waiting for an answer.

'Well, I reckon I've been doing the wrong thing by you, dragging you around the bush. You need a roof over your head, you need to be learning a trade, getting an education, not messing around with a useless old man like me. I'm taking you north. There's a station, Tara Downs, they could use a boy like you. Old friend of mine runs it. If I asked, they'd have a place for you there, send you to Katherine or Darwin to school, maybe get you an apprenticeship on the station one day.'

'But you said we should stick together.' Colm stared angrily at the crumpled paper in Bill's hand. 'What was in that letter?' he asked.

'None of your business,' said Bill, 'Just my past catching up with me, and that's nothing you need to know about.'

When the waiter brought the beer over, Bill ordered a big breakfast of bacon, eggs and baked beans for Colm even though he said he wasn't hungry. Colm pushed the beans around the plate and then mashed them hard with his fork.

19 Into the flames

....

They left Alice Springs later that morning. Bill gave the mechanic an extra five pounds to hurry the work on Tin Annie while he shopped for supplies. Colm sat with Rusty under a tree on the banks of the Todd River, waiting. The
5 river was dry and small groups of Aboriginals sat around campfires in the sandy bed. Colm drew his knees up against his chest and watched them. When he shut his eyes, he could picture the evenings around the fire with Doreen and Rosie back in Kalgoorlie. He thought of the
10 nights in the desert, watching the *Yartooka* bright above them. It didn't seem to matter how brave you were, bad things could come and change your life in a minute, ruin your dreams. He had thought he'd be travelling with Bill for ever. And now Bill was talking about getting rid of him.
15 The world had never felt so confusing.

The road north was smooth black bitumen, stretching through the desert. After the months of driving on corrugations, it was strange to hear only the humming of tyres on the road. The silence inside the car was so heavy
20 with unspoken thoughts that Colm wished for the noise of the rough desert tracks.

The landscape grew less familiar the further north they drove. Colm shut his eyes and thought of those long days when they drove with seemingly no direction. It used to
25 bother him that Bill never told him where they were headed, but now that they had a destination he wished he'd never heard of it. Tara Downs; if only it was at the other end of the Earth, instead of a few days away.

At sunset, they set up camp. Colm watched Bill pull another bottle of beer out of the back. He'd already drunk a bottle with breakfast and another at lunch.

'What are you looking at?' said Bill. 'Can't a man enjoy a quiet beer?'

'I didn't say anything,' said Colm.

'That's the problem with you, boy. You say everything when you say nothing.'

Colm watched him. All day he'd been thinking about what he could say that would change Bill's mind but he knew it was impossible to talk to the old man when he was drinking. When Bill opened his fourth bottle and was staring into the fire, Colm quietly took the bottle-opener from beside him. He walked across the red sand until he came to an ant-hill and then he dropped the bottle opener through a hole in the top. It was as easy as posting a letter. Rusty gazed up at him questioningly and he knelt down and patted her.

'That's fixed him,' said Colm. He knew Rusty didn't like it when Bill was drunk any more than he did. They tiptoed back to the campsite and he lay on his stomach in the dust, waiting. He hummed softly, a quiet, cheerful tune.

Bill began searching around amongst the supplies. Finally there was the sound of breaking glass. Colm moved a little closer. He saw Bill holding a broken bottle, staring at the glass. Bill poured a little of the beer into a tin cup, then seemed to change his mind. He threw the beer and the broken bottle into the darkness, and lay down with his blanket beside the fire.

When Colm thought Bill was asleep, he tiptoed into the ring of firelight and whistled softly for Rusty. He reached into his pocket and took out the picture of Blue Delaney.

Having her picture, like the picture of the Virgin, gave a focus for his prayers even though her face had become so familiar that he didn't need to see the crumpled photograph any more. If it was Blue Delaney's letter that had upset things, maybe praying to her could change things back to the way they were, and stop them from going to Tara Downs. He touched the photo to his forehead and let the prayers pour out of him and into the starry night.

There was a roar from across the campfire. 'What the hell are you doing?'

'I'm praying.'

Bill stood above him, casting a long shadow across Colm's body.

'What's that in your hand?'

'It's Blue Delaney. You know that,' said Colm, feeling the anger swell in him.

'Blue Delaney,' said Bill with anger in his voice. 'Give me that photo.'

Colm handed Bill the photo. Bill stared at it hard for a moment and then suddenly he threw it on the fire.

'What are you doing!' shouted Colm, trying to grab the picture from the flames. Rusty started barking but the photo quickly burst into flame, sending a glow of light across Bill's face.

'Why did you do that?'

'You don't need to be praying to Blue Delaney. She wouldn't like your prayers. She doesn't believe in God. Christ knows what she believes in.'

'You don't know that. You told me you don't know anything about her,' shouted Colm through his tears.

'You're right there, cobber,' said Bill. 'I don't know anything about her.'

He turned away and stumbled over to Tin Annie. Colm could hear him climbing into the cab.

Colm put an arm around Rusty and drew her closer. He didn't want to cry any more but the tears forced their way out, soaking Rusty's red fur.

The next day, Bill was even more silent than before. He didn't climb out of Tin Annie until long after sunrise, when the heat inside the cab became too much for him. He moved awkwardly, as if he was walking over broken glass, and every little sound made him wince.

Colm felt as if his chest was aching, as if all the tears he had cried had robbed him of his strength. He couldn't stop going over the events of last night. It would have been better if Bill had hit him, rather than burn the photo. He should have found the letter and burnt that instead. He should have done things differently.

Neither of them spoke a word during that day's long drive. Colm wound down his window and let the desert wind blow through the cab. He knelt on the seat with his back to Bill all the way north. In the evening, they sat silently around the campfire. Bill managed to open his beer on Tin Annie's wheels. Colm pulled out his harmonica, playing a slow, melancholy tune as Bill drank.

They drove into Pine Creek late on a Friday afternoon. Dozens of cars were parked outside the pub, and horses were tied to the rail. Inside, the smell of sweat and beer was thick.

Bill leant across the bar. 'Where can I find the boss? She in tonight?'

'She's out at Tara Downs,' said the barman.

'She?' asked Colm.

'Mrs Annie Mahoney.'

'She's the boss?' asked Colm. He couldn't imagine a woman as a boss of a big station and a pub.

'Bossiest woman I've ever known, I can tell you that,' said Bill.

5 'Did you name Tin Annie after her?' asked Colm, suddenly making the connection.

'You don't miss anything, do you? Don't you go calling this old heap of metal Annie in front of Mrs Mahoney. That's our little secret, that is.'

10 Colm felt hope. At least they could still share secrets. Maybe they were still a team.

....

They drove along a narrow track into the hills behind Pine Creek. Colm silently prayed for Tin Annie to break down before they got to Tara Downs, but she was as reliable as ever.

5 Suddenly the landscape changed. There were mango trees with golden fruit on them, and as they turned up the driveway they saw a huge banana tree with a giant hand of bananas hanging almost to the ground.

At the end of the driveway was a big white house. 10 Growing up one side of the building were thick green plants covered in flowers and strange fruits. Bill rang the bell. Footsteps echoed inside but it was some time before the door opened.

An Aboriginal woman in a dark dress stood there, 15 staring at Bill.

'You tell Mrs Mahoney Billy Dare and a friend are here to see her.'

The housekeeper disappeared and then Colm heard a shout that echoed down the empty hall. An older woman 20 stepped out from a doorway.

'Jesus, Mary and Joseph! If it isn't the old devil himself!' Colm didn't know old ladies could look so scary. She was tall for a woman, especially an old woman, and she had a mane of silver-white hair, and dark eyes. Colm couldn't 25 imagine her as a young girl in a blue dress. She looked as if she'd always been as she was right now.

The lady took Bill by both hands and led him into the living room, where she poured a golden liqueur into two small crystal glasses and offered one to Bill. Suddenly, she

became aware of Colm at last and she shouted into the hall, 'Jessie, bring us some soda for the kid!' Then she grabbed Bill by the arm and made him sit down on the big white couch. Red dust rose up around him. When Colm
5 went to sit beside Bill, Mrs Mahoney directed him to a chair to one side.

'We don't want to dirty the couch, do we?' she said. Colm wanted to point out that Bill was even dirtier than he was but somehow it didn't seem like a good idea.

10 'Billy Dare, back from the dead!' she said, sitting down beside him on the couch. 'Fancy you turning up like this, out of the blue. Why it must be fifteen years since you were here. You're lucky you caught me. Only came back last month. London, Paris and Rome and then business in
15 Singapore on the way south. Course, I've got a hotel up in Darwin that's doing good trade these days, so I'm there a lot of the time too.'

'How does Bert take to that?'

Mrs Mahoney put down her glass.

20 'Bert's no longer with us,' she said, reaching for the decanter.

'I'm sorry to hear it, Annie,' said Bill.

She looked up and smiled.

'You know I've never been very good at hanging onto
25 my men,' she said, looking at Bill over the her glass. Colm couldn't read her expression but he knew, straight away, that he didn't like her.

'So is there a number four on the horizon?' asked Bill.

Mrs Mahoney laughed. 'You up for grabs, Billy Dare?'

30 'You know Violet was the only girl for me,' he replied.

Violet? thought Colm. Who was Violet? In all the stories

he'd told, Bill had never said anything about someone called Violet.

Jessie brought in a tray with tiny biscuits, and a long glass of lemonade for Colm. Colm was desperate to get outside. The smell of the old woman's perfume was making him feel sick.

'I'd better see how Rusty's doing,' said Colm, interrupting the adults' conversation. Bill didn't even seem to notice as he left the room.

Out in the hall, he heard Mrs Mahoney's voice again. 'So the boy? He couldn't be a grandson. Doesn't look like a Delaney to me.'

'You don't think so?' said Bill. 'Ted Kelly reckoned he did. Reckoned he was like my Clancy.' Colm could hear the smile in his voice.

'He's an old fool. Always says what he thinks folk want to hear. That boy's nothing like Clancy.'

There was a short silence. Colm wished he could see Bill. It was always easier to read his expressions than the tone of his voice. When he finally spoke again, his voice was soft and low.

'He's not mine. But the boy, he's like an echo. You know, Annie, I lost Clancy. His plane went down over Borneo. Twenty-three years old and shot to pieces.'

'I'm so sorry, Billy.' There was a long silence. Their voices were so quiet Colm couldn't make out what they were saying. He was just about to tiptoe away when Mrs Mahoney spoke loudly again.

'But this boy, this Colin or whatever you called him?'

'Colm. He's an orphan. It's a long story. But I like the boy. He's the reason I'm here. I was wondering ...'

Colm didn't want to hear the rest, didn't want to hear Bill trying to make him stay with this crazy old lady. He was glad to get outside.

The sun was sinking low behind the banana palms. Colm walked amongst the strange trees, touching them, admiring the ripe fruit. He came to a long palm with huge green-and-black fruit at the top and tried to knock one down with a long branch he found in the grass. Then a girl appeared, stepping out from behind a banana palm. She had golden skin and shining black hair.

'You won't knock him loose like that,' she said.

Colm threw the stick on the ground. The girl came over and showed him how to climb the trunk.

'Will Mrs Mahoney mind?' asked Colm, glancing back at the house.

'They're not Mrs Mahoney's coconuts. My granny, she grows them.'

'Who's your granny, then?'

'Granny Hum Lee. She makes all these gardens. She's done it since she was a little girl. So I reckon she's the boss of it.'

'She works for Mrs Mahoney, doesn't she? Then they're Mrs Mahoney's coconuts.'

The girl stared at him without smiling.

'I'm Colm,' he said, stretching his hand out to shake hers.

'Lily,' she answered. 'Lily Yen Lin.' She took his hand. Her eyes were brown with little flecks of gold.

They sat in the long grass while Lily showed him how to take the skin off the coconut. Then she took out a knife and made a hole in the top.

'Here,' she said. 'Drink it. It's yummy.'

Colm took a deep breath and tipped the coconut back. The juice was warm and sweet. The taste was so unexpected that he almost spat it out, but he caught Lily watching him.

5 'It's good,' he said.

'I told you it was nice. Now we can eat the coconut meat.'

It was the strangest meal that Colm had ever eaten.

'Is Mrs Mahoney rich?' asked Colm as he chewed on a
10 piece of coconut. 'I mean, all this.' He waved his hands across the garden and the house. 'Did her husbands leave her lots of money?'

'Mrs Mahoney got rich all by herself. She's crazy but she's real smart too. Granny says she was the richest
15 woman in the Territory. They used to call her the Wolfram Queen.'

'What's wolfram?'

'They use it to make steel. She made lots of money during the First World War 'cause they needed lots of steel
20 for tanks and guns and things. But then she got tired of mining and bought cattle stations and hotels instead. Like I said, she's crazy. She owns everything.'

'Well, she won't own me,' said Colm, suddenly angry.

'She doesn't have slaves,' said Lily, rolling her eyes.
25 'And even if she did, why would she want you?'

'She doesn't want me,' said Colm. 'Nobody does.'

21   Wild boar country

Next morning Colm managed to stop Bill when he went out to the ute to see Rusty.

'Grandad,' said Colm, glancing over his shoulder to make sure Mrs Mahoney wasn't nearby. 'Grandad, please 5 don't make me stay here. Take me with you. And let's go soon. I promise I'll be good. I won't get in your way and I won't hide your bottle-opener or anything. I'll do everything you say.'

'I'm not in a hurry to move on. She does me good, that 10 old girl Annie. But when I do move on, you have to stay. Haven't quite talked Mrs Mahoney into the idea, but she'll see the sense in it soon. You ought to take an interest in the place. Get to know some of the jackeroos, they're great blokes, not keep hanging around the garden with that 15 little Lily. Listen, Colm, you need a proper home and a school where they can give you some book learning. Clancy, my son, he needed that too. Instead, I dragged him around the country with me. He missed out on all the ordinary things a boy should have: a mother, a home, a 20 good education.'

'I reckon he would have been happy, if he was travelling around with you.'

'You're staying here and I'm heading south again. That's the plan.'

25 'But Mrs Mahoney doesn't want me to stay here.'

'You don't know what that woman is thinking from one day to the next. You can go up to Darwin, go to boarding school up there during the term and come down and work on Tara Downs in the holidays. That's the sort of life Clancy should have had.'

'But it's not the sort of life I want to have!' said Colm. Bill stood up and dusted his hands, signalling the end of the conversation. 'C'mon. I've got a job to do. Can't sit around and talk all day. A wild boar's been making trouble just south a bit. They mess with the dams and the fences. Get in the ute and you can help.'

They drove out into the landscape where the old trees looked like burned bones. Tin Annie struggled over the dry creek beds and Rusty put her head out the open window, watching the fine red dust fly up around the sides of the ute.

'This is the place. We'll look for the boar on foot from here. You stay close by me.'

Colm followed Bill through the scrub. A hot, foul smell was in the air. As the smell grew stronger, Rusty put her head down and walked in front, as if she was following something. She led them to what was left of a steer. A cloud of flies flew up in the air.

Bill knelt down beside the dead steer. 'He's not long dead.'

They climbed up a nearby hill and scanned the countryside. Apart from a family of wallabies they could see nothing.

'Damn, he heard us.' Bill turned to walk back to the steer. There was a noise in the scrub and the black boar was on them. Colm jumped behind a rock as the boar hit Bill and sent him flying. It ran at the old man with its tusks, tearing his boot and ripping open his leg. Bill let out a cry of pain.

Blood poured from Bill's leg as the boar attacked again, and the old man struggled free. Rusty sank her teeth into the boar's leg but it turned and tore her with its tusks. Rusty yelped and fell.

5 Colm jumped out from behind the rock. He had to do something.

Bill was afraid. 'Run, Colm, get out of here,' he shouted. 'Get help!'

Colm turned and ran down the path. He had nearly got
10 to Tin Annie when he heard a terrible cry, more animal than human. He stopped and turned. What if Bill was killed before he could get help? What should he do? Run back to Tara Downs? Try to save Bill alone? Suddenly, he realised there was only one answer and there was no time
15 to lose.

He ran back to Bill. On the way he picked up a stick. As he came over the hill, he ran at the boar, hitting it again and again. It turned to face Colm. There was blood on its tusks.

20 Bill tried to pull himself away, leaving a trail of blood behind him. Colm raised the stick high and brought it down on the boar's head. The boar snorted, but instead of running at Colm, it turned back to Bill.

Colm threw the stick down and grabbed Bill's gun. He
25 was shaking as he raised the gun to his shoulder. Colm knew that if he shot the animal in the back, it would only make it wild. He let out a scream, a long, loud scream. The boar turned round. For a moment it stared at him. Then it lowered its head and ran towards him. Colm aimed straight
30 between the eyes.

The kickback from the gun made Colm stagger. He fell in the sand beside Rusty.

'Colm, my mate,' said Bill. He held out one bloodied hand and smiled. Then he lay back in the red dust and passed out.

Suddenly, everything was quiet. Blood soaked into the dry earth around Bill, in a dark circle. Colm could see the bones of his thigh where the boar had ripped open the flesh. He would have to stop the blood flow or Bill would bleed to death. Colm ran back to the ute and grabbed an old shirt to tie up the wound. Then he took off his own shirt and tore it up for Bill's hands. When he was sure the bleeding was slower, he sat back and tried to think. He had to get help, but how? The flies were gathering. He would have to get Bill into the car.

Colm took Bill's arms and put one over each of his shoulders and then tried to pull the old man up. It was almost impossible. He'd never be able to go a long way like this. He laid Bill down again and ran to Tin Annie. Colm took a deep breath and turned the key. Tin Annie started. He had no idea how to drive backwards, so he moved forward carefully, bringing the car as close to Bill as he could. Somehow, he found the strength to pull Bill back on his shoulders and put him into the car. Then he ran and picked Rusty up. He could just hear dog's heart beat and it gave him hope.

The dust flew up around the car as Colm raced along the track. Every time they hit a stone Bill cried out with pain, but at least that meant he was still alive.

When they drove across a dry creek bed, Tin Annie first struggled, then stopped. Colm tried to start her up again. But even as his foot pushed to the floor, he knew it was a mistake. The old ute died completely.

They were just at the top of the hill and he could see Tara Downs, but there was still at least a mile to go. He tried to start the car again and again, but it was no good. He would have to go on foot and leave Bill and Rusty in the car.

Colm wished the old man was conscious and could tell him what to do next. Then he began the long run to Tara Downs.

Colm's heart pounded and his head hurt, but the ground flew beneath him. He took the steps up to the house two at a time.

'It's Bill. An accident. He's bleeding, real bad. A boar ripped him up.'

Then Colm sank down on his knees. People appeared from nowhere. They ran, a car started up and strong arms helped Colm to his feet and took him into a bedroom. For a moment, he struggled against them. 'I have to be with Bill. He needs me,' said Colm.

'They're getting the Flying Doctor out here. We don't know if the old man will make it if we have to drive him down to the hospital in Katherine. Best to fly him to Darwin.'

Colm felt the blood drain from his face. 'He will make it. He has to make it.'

....

They loaded Bill into the light aircraft.

'Can I go too?' asked Colm.

'Sorry, sonny, no passengers,' said the medical officer. Mrs Mahoney and Colm watched the tiny plane take off into the blue sky, becoming smaller and smaller and then disappearing over the horizon. Bill was gone. The future was a dark hole.

'C'mon, boy. Don't stand around like a drongo. Get in the Bentley.'

'Where are you taking me?'

'We're driving up to Darwin. You don't want Bill waking up and finding we've abandoned him, do you?'

The night was black and moonless as the Bentley drove north. Compared to Tin Annie, the Bentley was like a space-ship, the leather smooth, the engine quiet as the night.

Finally, Mrs Mahoney spoke.

'You did a good job rescuing Bill.'

'I should have picked up the gun sooner.'

'You picked it up soon enough to save him. He could have bled to death. I worry about that old man. He needs to settle down in one place.'

'Are you going to make him marry you?' Mrs Mahoney shouted with laughter.

'I like the way you put that. No one has ever been able to "make" Bill do anything he doesn't want to. Stubborn as a mule and always has his own way in the end.'

'But he wanted me to stay with you,' Colm said. 'And he couldn't make you say yes, could he?'

I reckon Bill took you on 'cause he was trying to make history repeat itself. See, Billy was once a stray himself. My old auntie Bridie took him in and loved him as if he was her own, but then again, he was easy to love.'

5 She glanced across at Colm and he got the uncomfortable feeling that she didn't think he was lovable at all.

'When you get old, you start to realise that every good thing you do comes back to you – and most of the bad as well. Your grandad, he understands that.'

10 'He's not really my grandad,' said Colm in a small voice. 'And he wants to leave me behind. He wouldn't want to do that if I was really his grandson.'

The silence in the car grew heavy. Colm wished Mrs Mahoney would say something, tell him that of course Bill
15 was his grandad, of course Bill wouldn't leave him, but she kept her gaze on the road. Colm hummed a tune under his breath, trying to push away his fear. Suddenly, Mrs Mahoney spoke again.

'Don't you worry too much about old Billy Dare. No old
20 boar can finish him. Did you know me and Billy have been mates for more than fifty years? He's my lucky touchstone. As long as Bill's fighting his fights, I know I can go on battling, too.'

'If anything happened to Grandad … I don't know what
25 I'd do. He's all I've got.'

'Then we'll just have to make sure your "Grandad" survives, won't we?'

Colm smiled. For the first time, he understood what Bill liked about this bossy old woman.

30 It took hours for the lights of Darwin to appear on the horizon. Colm's head ached with tiredness. Inside the

hospital, the lights seemed bright and harsh after the darkness of the desert.

At the front desk, Mrs Mahoney announced that she and Colm were there to see Bill.

'I'm sorry Mrs Mahoney, but the boy can't come into the hospital. Children aren't allowed.'

'Don't be ridiculous,' said Mrs Mahoney. 'The boy's with me and he's here to see his grandfather.'

'You'll have to speak with the doctor, ma'am. Children are definitely not allowed.'

A nurse guided Colm out onto the verandah and he watched as Mrs Mahoney stood by the front desk, her face red with anger. She argued with everyone. Colm couldn't quite make out what they were saying, but Mrs Mahoney was definitely winning. Finally, the same nurse that had seen him out gestured for him to come back in.

'I'll cover whatever it costs,' said Mrs Mahoney briskly. 'And if you can't fix him up, find someone who can.'

'Mrs Mahoney, we're doing our best but his injuries are serious. He's lucky to be alive and he may never walk again.'

Colm's heart sank. 'Can I see Grandad now?' he asked.

'Sure,' said Mrs Mahoney. She led him down the corridors. 'They wouldn't let you on the men's ward, so I had him moved. Damn stupid rules they have here.'

All the nurses pretended not to see them as they turned into a small private room where a nurse was closing the windows against the night. Bill was covered with bandages. There was even one around his head and he seemed to be asleep.

Gently, Colm touched the tips of Bill's fingers with his own. If he concentrated, he could feel his prayers moving between the two of them.

'We're still a team, Grandad,' he whispered.

Bill's eyelids flickered and slowly, painfully, he opened his eyes. Mrs Mahoney stepped forward and touched his cheek. 'Billy, I've told them they have to set you right.'

He shut his eyes and went to sleep again. Mrs Mahoney gestured to Colm that they should leave.

'I'll be back, Grandad. I'll be back soon,' promised Colm. Mrs Mahoney guided him to the door. They were nearly out of the room when they heard Bill speak. 'Blue, need Blue. Me and the kid … talk to her.'

Mrs Mahoney returned to Bill's side. 'Billy, don't try to talk. You have to rest.'

'No, Annie. My Blue, my little Bridie. If I could … the chance . . ' His voice became weak.

Colm and Mrs Mahoney stood there, frozen.

'She wrote him a letter. Blue Delaney. She wrote to him when we were in Alice Springs,' said Colm, as they walked down the hospital corridor.

'Well, she is his daughter.'

Colm stopped. 'His daughter?'

Mrs Mahoney turned to Colm and smiled at his astonishment.

'But he was really upset,' said Colm.

'Oh, they've always fought like cats and dogs.'

Colm couldn't understand what Mrs Mahoney was talking about but he knew that whatever had been in the letter had changed everything. And now Bill had asked for Blue, and Colm knew that it was important.

'But he burnt her photo! He threw it on the camp fire! His own daughter!'

'Burnt her photo?' she echoed, frowning.

Mrs Mahoney drove to a hotel in the heart of Darwin. Neither of them spoke. Colm couldn't sleep, praying more than he ever had in his life.

At the breakfast table, Mrs Mahoney looked as though she hadn't had any sleep either. Colm could tell she'd put on extra face powder to cover the dark rings under her eyes. Later in the morning they went to visit Bill, but he was in a deep sleep and Mrs Mahoney had to have another argument with the nurse about bringing Colm into the hospital again.

'I'm sending you back to Tara Downs,' she announced, as they walked down the hospital stairs.

'No, I have to be near Grandad!'

'Don't tell me what to do, young man,' said Mrs Mahoney imperiously. 'I'll stay here in Darwin and keep an eye on him but I don't want you in my way.'

A truck taking cattle south picked Colm up later that morning and dropped him back at Tara Downs.

Rusty lay in a basket on the back verandah of the white house. Colm knelt down beside the basket and rested one hand gently on her head. Rusty's tail began to wag. When Colm stroked her, she licked his hand. Gently, he wrapped his arms around the dog and pressed his face against her.

'They should have put her down,' said Jessie the housekeeper. 'But that Lily, she's been up here taking care of her.'

The next morning, Colm went down to Lily's house. Lily was kneeling beside a patch of newly turned earth, planting something, when Colm called out to her

'Thanks for taking care of Rusty. I should have done that.'

She looked up and waved away his thanks. 'No, you had to be with your grandad. It must have been scary. I've been waiting for you to come back so I can give you this,' she said, shyly thrusting a small stone at him.

Colm held the stone up to the light. It was small and pale green, with a tiny dragon on one side.

'What is it?'

'It's for good luck. For your grandad.' Lily leant closer to him and pointed out the details. 'See, it's got a dragon on it because the dragon is for good luck and for a long life, so your grandad will get better and live a long time. It's got a Chinese symbol on the other side which means long life. Granny says that it gives a boy courage too, so we both thought you should have it. When you hold it tight, you can tell it works.'

Colm closed his hand over the pale green stone. Lily was right. The cool stone quickly grew warm in his hand. He slipped it into his pocket.

'Thanks, Lily,' he said. 'You want to go for a walk or something?'

Lily put away her garden tools and they headed out into the scrub. Colm told Lily all about the accident and what had happened in Darwin.

'I hate not being able to do anything. I hate being a kid. If I was older, they'd let me stay with him. If I was a man, Mrs Mahoney couldn't boss me around and leave me out of everything.'

'Don't you believe it!' said Lily, laughing. 'She wouldn't care if you were a man. She bosses everyone! The only person she can't boss is my granny. Who cares what Mrs Mahoney thinks anyway? She's not the boss of you.'

5   'I know. And I know Grandad needs me. I can feel it in my bones. I'm going to go back to Darwin and I don't care what Mrs Mahoney thinks.'

'Boy,' said Lily. 'That lucky charm works just like my Granny said it would!'

23 Flying south

Colm had made a plan, and he went to look for Lily to tell her about it.

'What are you going to do?' asked Lily.

'I'm going to hitch a lift back to Darwin with one of those cattle trucks.'

'Are you sure?' she asked.

Colm's answer was drowned out by Mrs Mahoney's Bentley, coated in dust from the long drive from Darwin. Colm marched up to her, his fists clenched.

'What you looking at me like that for?' she asked. 'You got a problem?'

'I have to go to Darwin,' he answered, hoping she wouldn't notice his shaky voice.

'Of course you do. Why do you think I drove all the way back except to collect you? You can pack up your things, and whatever you think Bill will want out of that old wreck of a car of his. You two have a plane to catch.'

Colm couldn't believe what he had just heard.

'Your grandad is pretty sick and I don't have time to nurse him myself,' said Mrs Mahoney angrily. 'So I'm sending him south. If it's the old boy's best chance of getting back on his feet, he'll have it. I've booked a nurse to go with you and a good place to take him in Melbourne and whatever else the doctors reckon he needs. The pair of you are catching the plane to Melbourne tomorrow.'

'But I don't understand,' said Colm. 'Grandad wanted me to stay with you.'

'Billy Dare may have been a great actor once but I can see straight through him. He may not be your real grandad, but he's fixed it in his mind that you belong to him.'

A warm feeling grew in Colm's chest. The stone in his pocket seemed to be warm too. He couldn't believe his good luck. 'But where will I live? They won't let me stay at the hospital, will they?'

'I've sorted that out too. Sent a telegram to Melbourne this afternoon. Bill came to for a while this morning and told me a few things. That letter that made him so wild, the one you told me about, it had news that his wife, Violet, died a couple of months back. First thing tomorrow morning, young man, you're flying south. South to Blue Delaney.'

Bill had been given sleeping tablets before they loaded him onto the plane. Colm stood beside Mrs Mahoney in the dawn light, holding the small suitcase of things that he'd packed for the journey south. Mrs Mahoney had bought him new clothes for the trip and he had made sure his hair was combed and his face clean so he would look his best.

Suddenly, everything seemed to be happening too quickly.

'What about Rusty?' he asked, turning to Mrs Mahoney.

'Don't you worry. Lily has been fussing over that dog for days. You've got enough to worry about, what with taking care of Bill and making sure that Blue Delaney behaves herself.'

'Behaves herself?' asked Colm.

'Blue's a good girl, even if she is full of mad ideas. This will change her, having to make peace with her father.'

'Is that why she changed her name? Because they fought?'

Mrs Mahoney smiled. 'No, Bill's real name was Patrick Delaney. Billy Dare was just his stage name. That's why his daughter is called Delaney.'

Colm couldn't believe they were talking about Blue Delaney, but at last, he knew Blue Delaney was a real person. A living person. And he was going to meet her. Mrs Mahoney had sent another telegram and written a long letter as well, which Colm was carrying in his jacket pocket.

'You take care of Bill,' said Mrs Mahoney. 'I know he means a lot to you but he means just as much to me.'

Colm shook hands with her and climbed onto the plane. He had never been in an aeroplane before and he sat in his seat feeling as though he'd left his stomach in Darwin. The roar of the engine filled his head with a noise that wouldn't stop.

All through the long dark journey, Colm thought about what lay ahead. What if the real Blue Delaney was nothing like the woman in the photo? What if he didn't recognise her? Maybe she was married now and had lots of kids – the last thing she'd want was another boy on her hands. Colm wanted to cry just thinking about it.

When the plane finally landed in Melbourne, the nurse and flight attendants were too busy looking after Bill to worry about Colm. He stood at the top of the steps, scanning the observation deck where a crowd of people stood watching the arriving and departing aeroplanes. There was a flash of red hair as a woman walked across the observation deck and disappeared into the airport terminal. He took a deep breath and walked down the steps.

....

The woman standing by the ambulance took one look at Bill and all the colour left her face. Colm recognised Blue Delaney straight away.

'That's her,' said Colm.

5 'Your aunt?' asked the stewardess. Colm nodded.

The stewardess took his hand and led him over to where Blue was standing.

'Mrs Delaney? Your nephew has been very good.'

'My nephew?' said Blue. Colm stared at her hard.

10 Blue turned to Colm and looked him up and down.

'Come along then,' was all she said.

For a moment, despite all the worry, despite all the terror of the last few days, Colm felt happy. Blue had her hand on his shoulder as they walked out of the airport and

15 into the bright morning sunshine. Anyone might think they were mother and son.

'You have a lot of explaining to do, young man,' she said as they watched the ambulance drive away with Bill inside it.

20 'Do you have any idea how difficult it was to get a hold of this car and come out to the airport to collect you? If it had just been Dad, I could have gone in the ambulance, but no, there's the pair of you to handle. Do you have any family in Melbourne that you can go to?'

25 Colm stared out at the city streets. There were so many people walking up and down the footpaths, marching in and out of buildings or waiting on tram stops, but he didn't know the name of a single one of them. The only person

in the whole city that he knew even the smallest thing about was Blue Delaney.

'Do you have a hearing problem? I asked if you have any family here in Melbourne.'

5   'I'm an orphan,' said Colm, hating the sound of the word.

'Perfect,' said Blue. 'An orphan. That'd be right. What was Annie thinking?'

Colm found himself wanting to defend Mrs Mahoney.
10 'She's paid for everything,' he said.

'Trust her to think money solves every problem!'

'She gave me this letter,' said Colm, pulling the envelope out of his jacket.

Blue glanced at it for a moment and then sighed.
15 'It always happens. Just when you think life is starting to go right, something comes along and messes you up.'

They stopped at a set of red lights. Colm had to fight down the instinct to jump out of the car and run away. He couldn't look at Blue Delaney. Even though she was just
20 like her photo in her pale blue coat and with red hair, nothing else about her was as he had expected. He took the dragon charm out of his pocket and held it tightly.

When they reached the hospital, Colm sat waiting on the steps while Blue filled in all the necessary forms and
25 argued with the doctors. Children weren't welcomed in this hospital any more than they had been in Darwin. Why did they treat him like that? He was the cleanest he'd been in months. He watched the traffic, the trams and people hurrying past. Compared to the bush, where everyone
30 wore working clothes, the people of Melbourne looked as if they were all on their way to a wedding. It all made his head spin.

When Blue came down the steps, Colm leapt up. 'Can I see him now?'

'You were with him all the way from Darwin. You don't need to see him.'

'I have to let him know I'm here,' said Colm.

'I promised Joe I'd bring his car back by three. Dad's fine and he knows you're with me so we're going, right now.'

As they drove away from the hospital, Blue glanced across at him. 'You don't have much to say for yourself, do you?' she said.

'I think a lot,' said Colm slowly, not sure how the words sounded.

'You and Dad must have made a strange pair, that's for sure,' she said shaking her head. Colm wondered if he should ask her exactly what she meant but he didn't know that he wanted to hear her answer. He had the feeling that arguing with Blue could be a dangerous business.

They drove into a long wide street with palm trees down the middle, and parked outside a tall house.

'Get out then,' she said.

'Is this where you live?'

'No, this is where the car lives. A friend of mine let me have it for a few hours,' she said. 'Now we have to catch the tram and the train back to Williamstown.'

A tall dark man stood on the balcony above them. 'Brigida!' he called.

Blue laughed. 'I told you I'd bring it back safely.'

'Wait, I'll drive you and your cousin back to your home!'

'Don't worry about it, Joe. I have to do a few things in town. I'll see you Friday night.' She held up the keys and dropped them into the letterbox, then quickly grabbed Colm and dragged him down the street.

5   'Why did you tell him I was your cousin?'

'I didn't tell him. Joe thinks everyone is everyone's cousin. He's Italian. He hasn't figured out about Australian families yet.'

'Is he your boyfriend?'

10   'No. He plays saxophone and sometimes I sing with his band. That's all. We're friends.'

'So should I call you Brigida, too?' he asked.

'You can call me anything you like,' she said.

25 Words and music

On the tram, Colm felt he was no longer in Australia. Australia was desert and sand, not a place of busy cities. He stared out at the old buildings, wide streets and green parks.

5   They were walking along Swanston Street when someone called out to Blue.

'You coming up for a cuppa, Blue?'

'We've got to get back to Williamstown before five,' said Blue.

10   'You've got plenty of time. Bring your young friend upstairs for some tea and toast.'

Colm followed Blue up the narrow staircase to a small café. Inside, there was a piano decorated with a vase of flowers. Colm wanted to sit down at the piano, but Blue
15   led him to one of the little tables. A man came and took their order and they sat opposite each other for the first time since he had arrived.

'Well, I guess I should read this letter before we go any further,' said Blue, when they each had a cup of hot tea in
20   front of them. Colm sat anxiously watching her read Mrs Mahoney's letter from beginning to end. When she'd finished, she turned the sheets of paper over and stared at the other side. Finally, she looked up at Colm.

'You've been travelling with Dad for over a year?' she
25   said, unbelievingly.

'A bit longer than a year. More like two, I think,' said Colm.

'And you call him Grandad?' she said

'He told me to,' said Colm.

'And you were on the road, all that time?'

'No, at first I lived with him in Fremantle but then … it was time to move on.'

'Time to move on,' echoed Blue. 'That's one of Dad's catchphrases for sure.' She started reading the letter from the beginning again, frowning as if it were written in another language.

Colm wanted her to look up from the letter and smile and say, 'Of course, if Bill is your grandad then you can be like a son to me, or at least my nephew!' Quietly he left his seat and went to the piano. He ran his fingers over the keys, careful not to press them though he could almost hear the notes inside his head. He hummed softly to himself as his fingers touched the black and white keys. Almost unconsciously, his hands formed the chords that he had played over and over in the asylum.

'Can you play?' asked Blue, coming up behind him.

'A little,' said Colm.

'Play me something. Something short.'

Colm sat down in front of the piano and shut his eyes. He began to play. He was relieved to discover that his fingers found their way to the right keys.

'You have a nice tone,' said Blue. It was the first time he had heard some kindness in her voice. She sat down beside him and played a few chords, and then suddenly she was humming and playing a piece of jazz. Colm watched her hands. When she played the refrain for a second time, he pulled out his harmonica and played along.

'You're very musical,' said Blue. 'Let's try another.'

This time, Colm picked up the tune even more quickly. Everyone in the café stopped what they were doing to watch the performance. When Blue started singing, her voice was so beautiful Colm shut his eyes and let the music wash over him. When the song was finished, everyone in the café broke into applause. Colm turned to Blue.

'Can you teach me to play that?' he asked.

Blue's expression grew sad. 'Somebody will teach you. You know Mrs Mahoney wants to pay for you to go to school? Some place called St Finian's College.'

'What if they find out where I came from?'

'Annie reckons she's got connections there, so I guess she knows what she's doing. I just hope to God it's a boarding school.'

'But aren't I going to live with you? Until Grandad gets out of hospital, that is.'

Blue looked up at him as if he'd suddenly grown two heads. 'We have to get going. We'll miss our train,' she said abruptly.

Colm wished they could go back to playing the piano. He had a feeling music might be a much better language to talk to Blue with than words.

Next morning, Colm was woken early by Blue. He had slept on an old brown couch in her living room, and his neck was stiff when he sat up. He shivered as he threw off the blankets. He'd forgotten what it was like to be cold
5   after months in the north.

Blue was making tea in the tiny kitchen. 'Quick, get some brekky into you. You're starting at St Finian's today.'

Colm put the box of cereal down and stared at her. 'But what about Grandad?'

10   Blue winced. 'Do you have to call him Grandad?'

'That's what he told me to call him.'

'Well, you can't see him today. He needs time to recover from the trip, and you need to start school.'

St Finian's was an old building on a busy street north of
15   the city. Outside, a group of boys in dark blue uniforms were gathering for assembly.

'Blue, I don't have a uniform,' said Colm.

'It won't matter for your first day,' said Blue. 'The important thing is to get you started.'

20   Colm knew she meant the most important thing was to get rid of him. As he waited for a student to take him to his first class, Blue said, 'Looks like you and me are stuck with each other for a while.' She drew an old envelope out of her handbag and scribbled a map on the back. '92 Flinders
25   Lane. That's where I'll be this afternoon. You catch the tram into town and then walk down this street here. It's where we got on the train yesterday.'

'What if I get lost?' said Colm.

'You're a big boy. You'll sort it out,' said Blue.

After school, it took Colm nearly an hour to decode the map that Blue had drawn for him. Outside 92 Flinders Lane there was a small sign with an arrow on it pointing to an entrance and the words 'New Theatre'. It didn't look very 'new' to Colm.

From above came the sound of music and singing and when he entered the hall he discovered a crowd of people dancing around on a stage. In the middle of the stage danced Blue, her long red hair like a flame.

When the music stopped, Blue spotted Colm and jumped down off the stage.

'So how'd it go?' she asked.

'It was all right,' said Colm. 'But can we go and see Grandad?'

Blue looked annoyed. 'It's too late now… Look, I telephoned this morning and he was doing fine.'

Every day that week and into the next, Colm met Blue after school at the New Theatre. Every day he asked when they were going to see Bill, and every day Blue would say, 'Look, don't worry, he's fine.'

'Did he ask after me? Didn't he ask to see me?' Colm asked.

One evening, Blue had left early to sing somewhere in the city. Colm was supposed to be asleep by the time she came home, but he was angry. Why wouldn't she take him to see Bill? When he heard footsteps on the stairs, he threw a blanket over himself and pretended he was asleep.

Blue and Joe tiptoed into the flat. Colm kept his eyes shut tight as they went into the kitchen. He heard the sound of Blue setting the kettle to boil. When he opened his eyes, he could see the two of them sitting at the table. 'Sorry about having to keep it quiet,' said Blue in a loud whisper. 'Won't be for much longer. I've written to the old woman asking her to fix it so he can go to boarding school.'

'I thought you liked him,' said Joe.

'Sure, I like him. He's not a bad kid. It's just I'm not cut out for this. The boy needs a proper family.'

'And he'll find this in a boarding school?' asked Joe.

'He'll be better off there than he is here'

'Is this what he thinks?' said Joe.

'Christ, Joe, I don't have any idea what he thinks. The only thing he ever says to me is "When can I see Grandad?"'

Joe lit a cigarette and thought. 'Isn't that good? That he wants to see the old man?'

Blue sighed. 'I've promised the kid I'll take him soon, but I don't reckon I can face it.'

'But he's your father, Brigida,' said Joe.

'We hadn't spoken in years. He can barely stand the sight of me.'

Colm couldn't listen any more. He threw off the blankets and marched into the kitchen. Joe and Blue looked up at him, startled.

'It's not true,' he shouted at Blue. 'He wanted to come to Melbourne just to be near you. He wanted to make it up to you, and you won't let him! Grandad needs us, Blue. He needs us now!'

Colm ran out of the kitchen, threw himself onto the old couch and pulled the blankets over his head.

Colm didn't know what Joe said to Blue but whatever it was, it worked. The next day Blue took Colm to visit Bill. It wasn't easy getting him past the nurse. The moment he was sure the nurse wasn't watching, he slipped through the door and followed Blue up the stairs.

Bill was sitting up in bed. His face was pale and he looked thinner and smaller than Colm remembered.

'Hello there!' said Bill.

'Grandad,' said Colm.

Colm stepped forward and took Bill's hands quickly between his own.

'I've been waiting for you, mate,' said Bill. 'It's good to see you.'

Colm glanced nervously over his shoulder at Blue, who stood by the door, looking as if she wanted to leave already. Bill glanced in Blue's direction too and then shut his eyes.

Blue coughed. 'I'm just going out for a cigarette,' she said. 'It doesn't look like you two need me around while you're talking.'

Bill opened one eye and watched Blue leave.

'So that Blue of mine, she's all right?'

Colm nodded.

'I hear that tricky old Annie Mahoney has you all signed up at St Finian's.'

Colm was surprised to hear himself say, 'I like it there. I pray for you every day, Grandad.'

'I don't understand it,' said Bill, shaking his head. 'They beat you within an inch of your life back in Bindoon and Clontarf, and here you are saying your prayers every day.'

'Everyone has to believe in something. Besides, my prayers have worked sometimes. Like when Rusty was poisoned, and when I thought I was never going to meet Blue, but now I have.'

'Well, you keep praying for me, mate.'

'Blue wants me to go to boarding school.'

'You call that girl back in here.'

'Please don't talk to her about it.'

'Call her, Colm.'

When Blue came back into the room, Colm wished he hadn't said anything.

'Is it too much to ask that you bring the boy to see me? Too much to ask that you show him a little bit of kindness?'

Suddenly, Blue stood up. 'Don't talk to me about kindness, Dad. I don't want to hear it. Where were you when Mum was dying?'

Bill grew quiet. 'I didn't know, Blue. You only wrote to me when she was already gone. I would have come back, if I'd known.'

'But you were always away! You were never around when we needed you. I needed you! Do you know what it was like, growing up without you there? You never thought about how it was for me!'

'Stop it!' Colm shouted, stepping between Blue and her father before she could say another word. 'Leave him alone!'

There was a noise in the corridor and suddenly a nurse was standing in the doorway.

'What is going on in here?' she said angrily. 'This isn't visiting hour, and even if it were, children are not allowed in the ward. The old gentleman needs his rest. His wounds will never heal. He needs to be left in peace.'

Colm looked from the old man to Blue. In a way, she looked as hurt as Bill.

Despite the fact that the cranky nurse complained, Blue arranged for Colm to visit Bill twice a week from then on. Colm had to catch two trams and a train and they wouldn't let him inside the hospital, but they would allow Bill to be wrapped up in blankets, placed in a wheelchair and then taken out onto the front porch.

Every visit, Bill asked after Blue. Colm would try to think of everything she'd been doing, but Bill always looked sad when he heard about her.

'Isn't she visiting you, Grandad?'

'If you can call standing in a corner of my room for five minutes a visit, I reckon I see her once a week,' he said.

Colm quickly tried to change the subject.

As the weeks went by, Colm started to feel that each time he went to see Bill, there was a little less of him there, as if the old man was disappearing. Sometimes Bill was too unwell to be brought out onto the porch and other times the visit had to be cut short because Bill would start to cough. Slowly, Colm began to realise that Billy Dare was dying.

One Sunday, Colm got up before Blue and headed out into the bright, cold morning. He ran down the street to the Catholic church. He knelt and prayed with all the concentration he could find. Next, he tried the Anglican church, the Methodists, the Baptists and even the Salvation Army.

....

Colm whistled cheerfully as he took the steps up to the flat two at a time. Blue had promised they could get fish and chips for tea that night. She was always in a better mood on the nights they bought takeaway.

5   Blue was standing by the window, looking down over the street. When she turned on Colm, her green eyes were angry.

'Colm, I've heard that you've been running around the streets on a Sunday morning attending every bloody 10 church in Williamstown. Can you explain yourself?'

'There's nothing wrong with going to church!' said Colm.

'One church, maybe, but six?'

'I only want to help Grandad. I don't know what else 15 to do. But it's not my prayers that he needs. He needs to see you.'

'He's got along fine without me for years. He can get well without me.'

'But Blue, he's not going to get well. Ever.'

20   'You're just a child. You can't know these things. He's got years in him yet.'

Colm shook his head. How could a grown-up be even better at pretending than any child?

'Everyone can see it, except you.'

25   All the colour left Blue's cheeks. He wanted her to be angry again, he wanted her to shout at him. Anything was better than her silence. 'Are you all right?' asked Colm, almost dreading the answer.

'No, I'm not. Everything, everything is falling apart.'

For a moment, he thought Blue was going to throw something at him, but she simply got up from her chair and left the flat. He watched her walk down Nelson Place and cross the road. There was something so small and
5 broken about her that he wished he could run after her and tell her he was going to make everything all right. But he didn't know what he could do, and their argument hung in the flat like a cloud of unhappiness.

He didn't hear the footsteps coming up the stairs.

10 'Oi,' said Joe. 'Where's Blue?'

'I said something she didn't like and it made her mad.'

Joe laughed. 'You're a good man, Colm. Whatever you said, she probably needed to hear it. But we'll bring her round, you and me. You can't be expected to take care of
15 Blue all on your own.'

'She thinks she's taking care of me,' said Colm.

Joe laughed. 'So what was it that she didn't want to hear?'

Later, when Blue returned, Colm left her and Joe alone
20 and sat on the steps of the flat, waiting. Joe was talking to Blue. No one had ever told him having a mother could be such hard work.

'Okay, Colm,' said Joe, opening the door of the flat and calling down. 'Grab your coat. You're going for a drive.'

25 No one spoke on the way to the hospital. Joe dropped Colm and Blue outside and then drove off into the night.

'It's not visiting hours,' said Blue.

'We're here now,' said Colm, taking her hand. They walked up the steps of the hospital together.

30 'Visiting hours are over. And Colm knows that children aren't allowed in the rooms or on the wards,' said the nurse at the desk.

'Oh, not this again. He's not a child.' said Blue. The nurse looked startled but she let them through without another word of protest.

Colm felt his heart sink when they walked into the room. Bill seemed even worse than the last time Colm had seen him.

'Grandad?' said Colm, touching Bill's hand. 'We're both here with you now. Me and Blue.'

'Blue and my cobber,' said Bill, smiling weakly.

Blue stood a little way away from them. Colm turned around and frowned at her.

'Don't you look at me like that, Colm McCabe. I'm here, aren't I?'

'Stand here,' said Colm, 'Where he can see you.' Blue came a little closer to the bed and Bill smiled.

'My little Bridie,' he said.

Blue put her hand to her mouth, as if to stop herself from saying something she would regret. Then all of a sudden she was crying.

'Come here,' said Bill. Slowly, Blue lay down on the bed beside her father. He put his arms around her and stroked her hair.

'Blue,' was all he said but the word was full of love. Colm stepped away, walking backwards quietly until he reached the door.

'Don't go, cobber,' said Bill slowly. 'Stay. Blue needs you. Stick together. Delaney and McCabe – a team.'

They sat by his bed all night. Colm fell asleep in his chair with his head resting on the side of the bed. He woke in the small hours of the morning. Bill's breathing had changed. Blue had fallen asleep too and her thick red hair was spread out across the bed. Colm touched the old man's hands but they had no warmth in them.

'Blue, wake up,' he said.

She rubbed her eyes, understood the situation, and then got to her feet. 'I'll get the nurse.'

Colm knelt down on the cold linoleum and prayed for Bill. He could see the life leaving the old man. Where was it going? — all that life force, all that energy, all that magic? Colm looked up at the face on the pillow and knew that Billy Dare was slipping away from him.

'Grandad,' he said. 'Grandad. Please don't be dead.'

But Billy Dare was gone.

The funeral procession moved slowly along the paths of the cemetery. Colm felt as if it should be raining, but it was a bright, sunny morning and the sun shone down on the mourners. Colm pulled out his harmonica. He closed his
5 eyes and played every tune Billy Dare had ever taught him.

Finally Blue put her hand on Colm's arm.

'Colm,' she said softly. 'It's time to go.'

Colm bent down to pick up a flower, a small daisy that
10 one of the mourners had dropped. He let it fall into the grave. It landed softly, white against the brown earth.

In the evening, Blue went down to the fish-and-chip shop while Joe and Colm walked to the end of the pier and watched the sun sink low over the bay.
15   'You're allowed to be sad about your grandad dying,' said Joe.

'He wasn't my grandad really,' said Colm. 'If he was really my grandad, then I'd be Blue's son or at least her nephew.'
20   'You're important to her, mate. She's changed since you've come to Melbourne.'

'But everything's dark. I can't see the future. I can't see what's going to happen next.'

Joe turned Colm to face him and looked hard into his
25 eyes. 'Look at it this way, mate, life is a little bit like the Olympic Games. You know how they light the flame to start, light it from a ray of sunshine all the way over in Greece? Then they guard that flame and make sure it stays

alight. They keep that flame burning until the last race is run. And when they're running, those athletes aren't enemies, they're brothers.'

'I don't understand,' said Colm.

5   'Well, you and Blue, you're on the same team but sometimes you both act like you're on opposite sides. She's trying to keep that flame alight too. Inside you, there's a flame and you gotta keep it burning bright. For you, for Blue, for your old grandad. That's what he would have
10 wanted. For both of you. *Capiche?'*

Colm put his hand over his chest and felt his own heart beating beneath. He tried to imagine a flame inside him, a flame so big it would keep the darkness at bay for ever.

One evening, after Blue and Colm had been out for fish and chips, Blue tousled Colm's hair. 'I reckon it's time we had a serious discussion about the future.'

'Can't we talk about this when we get back to your place?' said Colm, not looking her in the eye.

'Well, that's what I wanted to talk to you about,' said Blue.

Colm felt his heart grow heavy. She was putting him in a boarding school or sending him to a children's home.

'We can't go on staying in Williamstown,' said Blue.

'I know,' said Colm. He didn't want to hear what Blue was going to say next.

'I got a letter from Mrs Mahoney. She's sending Rusty down to Melbourne on the train from Alice Springs.'

'What?'

'She's sending Rusty and all Dad's things, including that wreck of a car, down to Melbourne. She thought I should have the old car and you should be taking care of Rusty. He's too old to be a working dog and she said she was tired of wasting good meat on him. So that means we can't stay in Williamstown. I'm not allowed to have pets in the flat. And you can't go on sleeping on the couch for ever either. So I've found us a house.'

'What?' repeated Colm. He couldn't believe what he was hearing.

'Would you stop saying "What?" It's rude. Say "pardon."'

'Pardon!' said Colm. He was looking at her hard now.

'I've found a house. Mum left me a little bit of money and it turns out Dad had a few hundred pounds.'

'You want me to stay with you?'

Blue looked at him nervously. 'I don't want you to go thinking I can be like your mum. But, if you can put up with me, I'd like it if … if we could work things out.'

Colm pinched himself hard on the arm, hard enough to leave a small bruise.

'What are you doing?' exclaimed Blue, stopping him.

'I just wanted to make sure I wasn't dreaming.'

Colm couldn't believe they were really going to have Rusty back. Tin Annie had arrived first and Blue had driven the old ute to Spencer Street Station to meet Rusty's train.

When the porter stepped out of the train with Rusty on a red leash, Colm had to look twice to recognise her. She looked so clean, not the dusty desert dog that Colm remembered. He knelt down and pressed his face into the red fur, remembering all the nights he and Bill had camped out in the desert with the night sky above them. In his mind's eye he could see Bill sleeping peacefully under that sky with the old dog at his side. He hugged Rusty tight. She licked his face so hard he had to let her go.

Blue and Colm's new home was a simple house with the paint coming off the front. Colm led Rusty up the narrow concrete path and proudly showed her every room. There were only four of them but Colm couldn't imagine wanting more.

Life in Newport was a new beginning for all of them. There were so many things that Blue and Colm could share, from walking Rusty together in the early mornings to planting a vegetable garden in the tiny back yard.

Now that they had a real kitchen, Blue decided she wanted to cook proper meals for both of them. Colm had to help while Blue read through the pages of the *Woman's Weekly*, studying the recipes section with a frown. Sometimes, he had to work hard to think up nice things to say about Blue's experiments. Even Rusty looked worried by the leftovers that found their way into her bowl.

On a long, hot summer evening a few days after Christmas, Blue pulled out a bottle of lemonade from the icebox and gave it to Colm. Then she made herself a drink and handed Colm a pair of folding chairs.

'Where are we going?' asked Colm, as Blue opened the front door and stepped outside with her drink.

'Come and see,' she said.

They walked down to the bottom of the street together where a crowd of neighbours were gathered, setting up deckchairs on the footpath and on the lawn of number 17. The family who had bought the first television on the street brought it out onto their verandah. Colm and Blue hardly knew their new neighbours but they quickly felt at home once the television was warmed up and they'd settled down in their deckchairs to watch the evening programs.

As they walked back home in the dark, Blue put her arm around Colm's shoulders.

'We're turning into a real pair of local yokels, you and me,' said Blue.

'That's not so bad,' said Colm.

'Maybe, but we're not staying in for New Year's Eve. I'm singing with Joe's band at a dance over in Carlton and you're coming along.'

'I thought you said they don't like having children at those dances.'

'You don't look like a little kid anymore. Look at the size of you! You're taller than me already! Besides, 1956 has been a big year for you and me, kiddo. I think we should see it out with a bang.'

On New Year's Eve, Colm sat at a table reserved for the band while Blue sang for a crowd of slow-dancing couples. '*Que sera sera*, whatever will be will be, the future's not ours to see …' Colm hummed along. The future wasn't his to see, but what he could see of it was looking brighter all the time.

Joe took a break and came and sat with Colm at their small table near the bandstand. He laid his saxophone beside them and sat back in his seat with a grin on his face. Then he reached into his pocket and took out a small blue leather box.

'So what do you reckon?' he asked, setting the box down on the table in front of Colm. When he raised the lid, Colm laughed. Inside was a gold ring with a sparkling pale green stone.

'What's so funny? You think she won't like it?'

'No, she'll like it, no worries,' said Colm.

'You know why I bought it then,' said Joe. 'I'm going to marry that girl. How do you feel about being best man at the wedding, eh?'

Colm laughed again. His chest almost ached with happiness.

Blue's voice sang out. '*Que sera sera*, whatever will be will be, the future's not ours to see …' Colm shut his eyes and said a prayer of thanks for Blue Delaney.

Author's note

....

This is a work of fiction, but many of the events are based on fact. Australia has had a long history of child migration schemes. After World War II, thousands of orphans were shipped to Australia from the UK, often against their will. Many of these children suffered unspeakable hardship and cruelty at the hands of those who were meant to care for them. Colm, Tommy and Dibs are imaginary boys but their experiences are based on those of real boys who participated in orphan migration schemes. In creating the fictitious characters that live within the pages of this novel, I drew on many sources. Although some of the characters are composites of real people, only Brother Keaney is an actual historical figure. An Irish ex-policeman, Brother Keaney was head of the Christian Brothers' home at Bindoon in the 1940s and 1950s.

While thousands of immigrant children were being sent to Australia, Aboriginal children were taken by force from their families, and put into institutions. It is ironic that in an age that celebrated the ideal of the family unit, so many children should have been forced to grow up in institutions.

History is never a single narrative, but a rich tapestry of interwoven stories. In choosing the historical threads to weave into *A Prayer for Blue Delaney*, I found the colour and vibrancy of the red heart of Australia irresistible. The stories of the Chinese in the Northern Territory, the sufferings of the Aboriginal stolen generations, and the idealists who challenged the traditional norms of culture in the 1950s were all historical elements that demanded a place in Colm's story.

Acknowledgements

In researching the 1950s I was able to draw on the observations and reflections of countless friends and acquaintances. To those many people who enriched this story and whose names are not listed below, thank you. I am especially grateful to the following people for their time, advice and inspiring suggestions: Lyn Ainslie, Mailee Clarke of the Fremantle Children's Literature Centre, Henry Paterson Finch, Nano Finch, Peter Freund, Leigh Hobbs, Ruby Hunter, Gaye Lawrence of Green Valley – Pine Creek, Gladys Elsie Sumner, Ann Tregear, Helen Tregear, and Gabrielle Wang. Also thanks to Sarah Brenan, Eva Mills and Rosalind Price for their wise editorial guidance.

All historical fiction is built on a foundation firmly laid by other writers and historians. I would particularly like to acknowledge the works of Alan Gill and Barry Coldrey in making it possible for me to reconstruct the experiences of the boys of Clontarf and Bindoon. Two separate Senate Committee inquiries produced reports that also assisted my research: *Lost Innocents: Righting the Record, The Report of the National Inquiry into Child Migration* and *Bringing Them Home, The Report of the National Inquiry into the Separation of Aboriginal and Torres Strait Islander Children from Their Families*. Both provided chilling factual information that influenced the creation of this novel.

David Unaipon's *Legendary Tales of the Australian Aborigines* provided a source for the legend of the *Mungingee*. The Ngarrindjeri woman who befriends Colm, Doreen, is fictional, but the details of the dreaming she tells are true and belong to the Ngarrindjeri people.

Mayse Young's autobiography, *No Place for a Woman*, and Barbara James's history, *No Man's Land – Women of the Northern Territory*, proved to be invaluable resources in writing the scenes set in Pine Creek. *The Dog Fence* by James Woodford provided many of the factual details incorporated into Colm and Bill's journey. The fragments of poetry that Bill recites to Colm include William Butler Yeats' 'Easter 1916' and Henry Lawson's 'The English Queen'.

For facilitating the research process, I would like to thank the Caroline Chisholm Library, the State Library of Victoria, Yarra Plenty Regional Libraries and the Performing Arts Museum, Melbourne. I would also like to acknowledge the support of the Australia Council for their initial funding, without which I would never have dreamt of attempting this series.

And to my family – Ken Harper, Ruby, Billy and Elwyn Murray and Isobel, Romanie and Theo Harper – thanks for your enduring support.

Vocabulary

A

(to) **abandon** [ə'bændən]
aufgeben, verlassen

according (to) [ə'kɔːdɪŋ] gemäß,
entsprechend

ain't [eɪnt] *(infml)* = am/is/are
not

ancient ['eɪntʃənt] uralt

apprenticeship [ə'prenɪʃɪp]
Lehre, Ausbildung

apricot ['eɪprɪkɒt] Aprikose

ashamed ['əʃeɪmd] beschämt

(to) **astonish** [ə'stɒnɪʃ]
erstaunen, überraschen

astonishment [ə'stɒnɪʃmənt]
Erstaunen

asylum for the insane [ə'saɪləm]
Irrenanstalt

aware [ə'weə(r)] bewusst,
bekannt

B

bait [beɪt] Köder

bandage ['bændɪdʒ] Verband

barbed wire [ˌbɑːbd 'waɪə(r)]
Stacheldraht

bare [beə(r)] nackt, kahl

barefoot ['beə(r)fʊt] barfuß

(to) **bark** [bɑːk] bellen

bark *(n)* Gebell

battered ['bætəd] abgenützt,
verbeult

(to) **beat** [biːt] schlagen

beating *(n)* ['biːtɪŋ] Schläge,
Prügel

(to) **beg** [beg] betteln

belt [belt] Gürtel

(to) **bend over** [ˌbend 'əʊvə] sich
bücken

Bentley ['bentli] *britische
Automarke*

best man [ˌbest 'mæn] Trauzeuge

(to) **billow** ['bɪləʊ] sich aufblähen

billycan ['bɪlikæn] *Metalldose, die
als Kochtopf verwendet wird*

bleeding *(adj)* [bliːdɪŋ] *(infml)*
verdammt

blow [bləʊ] *hier:* Schlag

boar [bɔː(r)] Wildschwein

boarding school ['bɔːdɪŋ ˌskuːl]
Internat

bossy ['bɒsi] herrisch

(to) **bother** ['bɒðə(r)] belästigen

bother *(n)* Ärger

brekky ['breki] *(AustralE)*
Frühstück

Brother ['brʌðə(r)]
Ordensbruder

bucket ['bʌkɪt] Eimer

bud [bʌd] Knospen

bulb [bʌlb] Glühbirne

bunch [bʌntʃ] Haufen

(to) **burst into tears** [bɜːst] in
Tränen ausbrechen

C

cab [kæb] Führerhäuschen

camp bed [ˌkæmp 'bed] Feldbett

cardboard tag ['kɑːdbɔːd ˌtæg]
Namensschild

carpentry ['kɑːpəntri]
Schreinerarbeiten
cart [kɑːt] Handwagen
(to) **catch a glimpse** (of sth.)
[kætʃ] einen flüchtigen Blick
(von etwas) erhaschen
catchphrase ['kætʃfreɪz] Motto
cattle ['kætl] Rinder
cemetery ['semətri] Friedhof
charge: (to) **be in charge**
(of sb./sth.) [tʃɑːdʒ]
(für jdn./etwas) zuständig/
verantwortlich sein
(to) **cheer sb. up** [tʃɪə(r)]
jdn. aufheitern
cheerful ['tʃɪəfl] fröhlich
chest [tʃest] Brust
(to) **chug** [tʃʌg] tuckern
(to) **clench one's fists** [klentʃ]
die Fäuste ballen
coat (of a dog) [kəʊt] Fell
cobber ['kɒbə(r)] (infml,
AustralE) Kumpel
(to) **complain** [kəm'pleɪn] sich
beklagen
concrete ['kɒŋkriːt] Beton
(to) **conquer** ['kɒŋkə(r)] erobern
(to) **cop it** [kɒp] (infml) bestraft
werden, dran sein
copper ['kɒpə(r)] (infml) Polizist,
Bulle
corrugation [ˌkɒrə'geɪʃn] Welle
(auf der Straße)
(to) **cough** [kɒf] husten
courtyard ['kɔːtkɑːd] Innenhof
cracker ['krækə(r)] (infml)
super-, spitzen-
cranky ['kræŋki] (AustralE)
launisch

crate [kreɪt] Kiste
(to) **crawl** [krɔːl] kriechen,
krabbeln
creek [kriːk] Bach, Fluss
crikey ['kraɪki] (infml) Mensch!
crumpled (adj) ['krʌmpld]
zerknittert

D

daft [dɑːft] blöd
damper ['dæmpə(r)]
australisches Busch-Brot
dashboard ['dæʃbɔːd]
Armaturenbrett
dawn [dɔːn] Morgendämmerung
deaf [def] taub
(to) **despair** [dɪ'speə(r)]
verzweifeln
despair (n) Verzweiflung
destination [ˌdestɪ'neɪʃn] (Reise-)
Ziel
dim [dɪm] trüb
dingo ['dɪŋgəʊ] australischer
Wildhund
discouraged [dɪs'kʌrɪdʒd]
entmutigt
(to) **disembark** [ˌdɪsɪm'bɑːk]
von Bord gehen
(to) **dive** (in) [daɪv] (ein)tauchen
done in (adj) [dʌn] (infml) fix und
fertig
(to) **drag** [dræg] schleppen
drongo ['drɒŋgəʊ] (AustralE)
Trottel
(to) **drown** [draʊn] ertrinken
dumb [dʌm] hier: dumm
dust [dʌst] Staub
dusty (adj) [dʌsti] staubig

E

Elders ['eldəz] Die Alten
envelope ['envələʊp]
  Briefumschlag
eventually [ɪ'ventʃuəli]
  schließlich
evil ['iːvl] böse
exhaustion [ɪg'zɔːstʃən]
  Erschöpfung
expression [ɪk'spreʃn]
  hier: Gesichtsausdruck

F

fairy-tale ['feəriteɪl] Märchen
familiar [fə'mɪliə(r)] bekannt
fault: (to) **be sb.'s fault**
  [fɔːlt] Schuld: jds. Schuld sein
favour: (to) **ask a favour**
  [feɪvə(r)] Gefallen: um einen
  Gefallen bitten
fella ['felə(r)] *(infml)* Kerl
fist [fɪst] Faust
fizzy ['fɪzi] sprudelnd
(to) **flail** [fleɪl] um sich schlagen
(to) **float** [fləʊt] schwimmen,
  sich auf dem Wasser treiben
  lassen
(to) **flog** [flɒg] auspeitschen
flogging *(n)* [flɒgɪŋ]
  Auspeitschung
forehead ['fɔːhed] Stirn
foul [faʊl] verdorben
frigging [frɪgɪŋ] *(infml)* verflucht
frog and toad [frɒg] [təʊd]
  (rhyming slang) = road
(to) **frown** [fraʊn] das Gesicht
  verziehen
fur [fɜː(r)] Fell, Pelz

G

(to) **gag** [gæg] würgen
gentle ['dʒentl] sanft
(to) **gesture** ['dʒestʃə(r)]
  Handzeichen geben,
  gestikulieren
(to) **get rid of sth.** [rɪd]
  etwas loswerden
(to) **giggle** ['gɪgl] kichern
gilt [gɪlt] golden, vergoldet
giveaway ['gɪvəweɪ]
  verräterisches Zeichen
git [gɪt] Blödmann, alter Sack
(to) **glance** (at sb./sth.)
  [glɑːns] (auf jdn./etwas) einen
  Blick werfen
(to) **glare (at)** [gleə(r)] wütend
  auf etwas schauen
(to) **glimpse:** (to) **catch a**
  glimpse (of sb./sth.)
  [glɪmps] (von jdm./etwas)
  einen Blick erhaschen
glimpse *(n)* kurzer Blick
(to) **glow** [gləʊ] glühen,
  glimmen
gob [gɒb] *(infml)* Maul
goer: (to) **be a goer** ['gəʊə(r)]
  (infml) nicht ohne sein
gooby eyes ['guːbiː] *(infml,*
  AustralE) Glupschaugen
grave [greɪv] Grab
graveyard [greɪvjɑːd] Friedhof
grin [grɪn] Grinsen
grinding wheel ['grɪndɪŋ ˌwiːl]
  Schleifrad
(to) **groan** [grəʊn] stöhnen
(to) **growl** [graʊl] knurren
gruel ['gruːəl] dünner Brei,
  Hafergrütze

grumpy ['grʌmpi] schlecht
gelaunt, mürrisch
guilt [gɪlt] Schuld
guts [gʌtz] *(infml)* Mut

H

(to) **hang on to sth.** [hæŋ]
sich an etwas klammern,
festhalten
harsh [hɑːʃ] Rau, grell
(to) **head for/towards sth.**
[hed] auf etwas zusteuern
hell [hel] Hölle
highway ['haɪweɪ] Landstrasse
hind legs [haɪnd] Hinterbeine
(to) **hitch a ride** [hɪtʃ] per
Anhalter fahren
(to) **hoist** [hɔɪst] hochziehen
housekeeper ['haʊskiːpə(r)]
Haushälter/in
(to) **hum** [hʌm] summen
instant ['ɪnstənt] Augenblick
intersection [ˌɪntə'sekʃn]
Straßenkreuzung

J

jackeroo [ˌdʒækə'ruː]
australischer Cowboy

K

(to) **keep a low profile** ['prəʊfaɪl]
unauffällig sein
(to) **keep an eye on sb./sth.**
jdn./etwas im Auge behalten
(to) **keep track of sth.** etwas
verfolgen
(to) **keep up with sb.** mit jdm.
Schritt halten

kelpie ['kelpi] *australische
Hundeart*
keys [kiːz] *hier:* Tasten
(to) **kneel** [niːl], **knelt, knelt**
knien
kookaburra ['kʊkəbʌrə]
australische Vogelart

L

lad [læd] Knabe, Junge, Bursche
lap [læp] Schoß
lawn [lɔːn] Rasenfläche
lean *(adj)* [liːn] hager, dürr
(to) **lean on** anlehnen
(to) **leap** [liːp] hervorspringen
leash [liːʃ] (Hunde-) Leine
(to) **leave off** [liːv] *(infml)*
aufhören
lilting [lɪltɪŋ] melodisch
limb [lɪm] Gliedmaße
(to) **limp** [lɪmp] hinken
(to) **load** [ləʊd] (be)laden
lock-smithing ['lɒksmɪθɪŋ]
Schlosserarbeit
lollies ['lɒliz] *(AustralE)*
Süßigkeiten
lot [lɒt] Menge
lousy ['laʊzi] *(infml)* lausig

M

(to) **make it** [meɪk] es schaffen
marbles ['mɑːblz] Murmeln
mass [mæs] (Heilige) Messe
mercy: (to) **be at the mercy of
sb.** ['mɜːsi] Gnade: jdm.
ausgeliefert sein
(to) **mess up** [mes] *(infml)*
versauen

(to) **mess with** *hier:* verarschen

(to) **mess around**
   hier: rumhängen

migrant ['maɪɡrənt] Migrant,
   Ein-/Auswanderer

(to) **mine** [maɪn] nach etwas
   graben, etwas abbauen

miserable ['mɪzrəbl] elend

mistletoe ['mɪsltəʊ] Mistelzweig

mob [mɒb] *(infml)* Bande

(to) **moor** [mɔː] vor Anker gehen

mound [maʊnd] Hügel

mourner ['mɔːnə(r)] Trauergast

(to) **muck around** [mʌk]
   herumblödeln

mule [mjuːl] Maultier

N

nut-house [nʌthaʊs] *(infml)*
   Irrenhaus

O

obstacle course ['ɒbstəkl ˌkɔːs]
   Hindernislauf

ocean liner ['əʊʃn ˌlaɪnə]
   Ozeandampfer

(to) **ooze** [uːz] heraussickern,
   triefen

orchard ['ɔːtʃəd] Obstgarten

out of the blue [aʊt] aus
   heiterem Himmel

outbreak ['aʊtbreɪk] Ausbruch

P

(to) **part** (from sb./sth.) [pɑːt]
   (von jdm./etwas) Abschied
   nehmen

(to) **pass out** [pɑːs] ohnmächtig
   werden, das Bewußtsein
   verlieren

passage(way) ['pæsɪdʒ(weɪ)]
   Gang

patron ['peɪtrən] Schutzheilige/r

pattern ['pætn] regelmäßige
   Vorgehensweise, Muster

peach [piːtʃ] Pfirsich

pillow ['pɪləʊ] Kopfkissen

(to) **pinch** [pɪntʃ] kneifen

plump [plʌmp] rundlich

polio ['pəʊliəʊ] Kinderlähmung

Pom (Pommy) [pɒm] *(infml,
   AustralE)* Engländer

porter ['pɔːtə(r)] Gepäckträger

porthole ['pɔːthəʊl] Bullauge

portico ['pɔːtɪkəʊ] Säulengang

possession [pəˈzeʃn] Besitz(tum)

(to) **pray** [preɪ] beten

prayer *(n)* [preə(r)] Gebet

(to) **pretend** [prɪˈtend] so tun, als
   ob

prospector [prəˈspektə(r)]
   Goldgräber

(to) **pull one's weight** [pʊl]
   Mithelfen, sich einsetzen

(to) **punch** [pʌntʃ] boxen

(to) **put down** [pʊt] *hier:* (ein
   Tier) einschläfern

R

race: 'the races'
   [reɪsɪz] Pferderennen

raw [rɔː] *hier:* wund

(to) **reckon** ['rekən] *(infml)*
   (aus)denken

records ['rekɔːdz] Akten

(to) **reek of sth.** [riːk] stark nach etwas riechen

reliable [rɪˈlaɪəbl] zuverlässig

reluctant *(adj)* [rɪˈlʌktənt] widerwillig

(to) **rest sth. on sth.** [rest] etwas auf etwas auflegen

rib [rɪb] Rippe

ridge [rɪdʒ] Bodenwelle

rifle [ˈraɪfl] Gewehr

(to) **rip** [rɪp] reißen, zerreißen

ripe [raɪp] reif

(to) **roar** [rɔː(r)] brüllen

roar *(n)* Gebrüll

(to) **rock** [rɒk] schaukeln, wiegen

(to) **round up** [raʊnd] zusammentreiben

S

Salvation Army [sælˈveɪʃn ˈɑːmi] Heilsarmee

scar [skɑː(r)] Narbe

(to) **scowl** [skaʊl] finster blicken

(to) **scratch** [skrætʃ] kratzen

(to) **scrub** [skrʌb] schrubben

scrub *(n)* Gestrüpp, Unterholz

self-conscious [ˌself ˈkɒnʃəs] unsicher, gehemmt

Seven Sisters [ˈsevn ˌsɪstəz] Plejaden (Sternbild)

shack [ʃæk] Hütte

shaft [ʃɑːft] Schacht

shame [ʃeɪm] Schande

(to) **shave** [ʃeɪv] (sich) rasieren

(to) **shoot up** [ʃuːt] emporschießen

shore [ʃɔː(r)] Ufer

(to) **shrug** [ʃrʌg] mit den Schultern zucken

shy [ʃaɪ] schüchtern

sight: in sight [saɪt] in Sicht

(to) **sin** [sɪn] sündigen

sin *(n)* Sünde

(to) **slap** [slæp] klatschen

(to) **slip** [slɪp] schlüpfen, stecken, schieben

(to) **snap** [snæp] schnappen; aggresiv antworten

(to) **snort** [snɔːt] schnauben

(to) **sob** [sɒb] schluchzen

Sonny Jim [ˈsʌni ˌdʒɪm] *(infml)* mein Junge

soothing [ˈsuːðɪŋ] beruhigend, besänftigend

(to) **sort (sth. out)** [sɔːt] (sich) um etwas kümmern

soul [səʊl] Seele

spark [spɑːk] Funke

spirit [ˈspɪrɪt] Geist

spiritual [ˈspɪrɪtʃʊəl] geistig

(to) **spit sth. (out)** [spɪt], **spat, spat** etwas (aus)spucken

(to) **stagger** [ˈstæɡə(r)] schwanken, taumeln

startled [ˈstɑːtld] überrascht

station [ˈsteɪʃn] *(AustralE)* Farm

steep [stiːp] steil

steer [stɪə(r)] (junger) Stier

(to) **sting** [stɪŋ], **stung, stung** stechen, brennen

(to) **strap** [stræp] mit einem Lederriemen schlagen

strap *(n)* Lederriemen

stray [streɪ] Straßenkind

(to) **stroke** [strəʊk] streicheln

(to) **struggle** [ˈstrʌɡl] kämpfen

stubborn ['stʌbən] stur

(to) **stumble** ['stʌmbl] stolpern

subject: (to) **be subject to sth.**
['sʌbdʒɪkt, 'sʌbdʒekt] etwas
unterworfen sein

superphosphate [ˌsuːpə'fɒsfeɪt]
Superphosphat (Kunst–
dünger)

supplies *(pl)* [sə'plaɪz] Vorräte

suspect [sə'spekt] verdächtigen

swag [swæg] *(AustralE)*
Schlafsack

(to) **swear** [sweə(r)], **swore,
sworn** schwören

T

(to) **talk sb. into doing sth.**
[tɔːk] jdn. überzeugen/
überreden, etwas zu tun

tarp [tɔːp] Abdeckplane

taste [teɪst] Geschmack

tear *(n)* [teə(r)] Träne

(to) **teeter** ['tiːtə(r)] taumeln

thermos ['θɜːməs]
Thermoskanne

(to) **thrash** [θræʃ] um sich
schlagen, (ver)prügeln

(to) **throw up** [θrəʊ]
sich übergeben

thunderous [θʌndərəs] laut,
zornig

tide [taɪd] Gezeiten, Ebbe, Flut

(to) **tingle** ['tɪŋgl] kribbeln,
prickeln

(to) **tiptoe** ['tɪptəʊ] auf
Zehenspitzen gehen

tool [tuːl] Werkzeug

touchstone ['tʌtʃstəʊn] Maßstab,
Prüfstein

trace [treɪs] Spur

(to) **trickle** ['trɪkl] tropfen,
tröpfeln

truck [trʌk] Lastwagen

(to) **trudge** [trʌdʒ] sich
dahinschleppen, stapfen,
trotten

tucker [ˌtʌkə(r)] *(AustralE)* Essen

tuft [tʌft] Büschel

tusk [tʌsk] Stoßzahn

U

uneasy [ʌn'iːziː] nervös,
unsicher, unentspannt

ungrateful [ʌn'greɪtfl] undankbar

up for: (to) **be up for sth.**
zur Verfügung stehen, bereit
sein, etwas zu tun

(to) **be up for grabs** *(infml)*
zu haben sein

upset [ʌp'set] traurig,
durcheinander

ute [juːt] *(AustralE)* eine Art Jeep

V

vast [vɑːst] ausgedehnt

W

(to) **wag** [wæg] wedeln

wagon: (to) **be on the wagon**
['wægən] *(infml)* abstinent sein

wallaby [wɒləbi] *australisches
Beuteltier*

(hospital) ward [wɔːd] Station

warily *(adv)* ['weərəli] vorsichtig

(to) **waste** [weɪst]
 verschwenden
waste *(n)* Abfall
(to) **watch out for sth.** [wɒtʃ]
 auf etwas aufpassen
way: (to) **have one's own way**
 seinen Willen durchsetzen
weathered ['weðə(r)d] verwittert
welfare ['welfeə(r)] Fürsorge
welt [welt] Schnittwunde
(to) **whimper** ['wɪmpə(r)]
 winseln
whinging ['wɪndʒɪŋ] sich
 beklagend, jammernd
(to) **whip** [wɪp] auspeitschen
whipping boy Prügelknabe
(to) **whisper** ['wɪspə(r)] flüstern
whisper Geflüster
whore [hɔ:(r)] Hure
wimple ['wɪmpl] Nonnenhaube
(to) **wince** [wɪns]
 zusammenzucken

windscreen ['wɪndskri:n]
 Windschutzscheibe
wing [wɪŋ] Flügel
(to) **wink** [wɪŋk] zwinkern
(to) **wipe** [waɪp] wischen
wire *(n)* ['waɪə(r)] Draht
wiry *(adj)* ['waɪəri] drahtig
wisp [wɪsp] Haarsträhne
(to) **wolf down** [wʊlf]
 herunterschlingen
wombat ['wɒmbæt]
 australisches Beuteltier
worn *(adj)* [wɔ:n] abgenutzt
wound [wu:nd] Wunde,
 Verletzung
(to) **wrap** [ræp] (ein)wickeln

Y
(to) **yell** [jel] schreien
(to) **yelp** [jelp] jaulen

Names

Alice Springs [ˌælɪs 'sprɪŋz]
Bindoon [ˌbɪn'du:n]
Ceduna [sə'du:nə]
Colm [kɒlm, 'kɒləm]
Clontarf ['klɒntɑ:f]
Clothilde ['klɒtɪld]
Darwin ['dɑ:wɪn]
Delaney [dəleɪni]
Dibs [dɪbz]
Doreen ['dɔ:ri:n]
Fremantle ['fri:mæntl]
Gnowangerup [nəwæŋgeɪ'rʌp]
Kalgoorlie [kæl'gʊəli]
Katanning [kə'tænɪŋ]

Kojonup ['kəʊdʒənəp]
Mahoney [mə'həʊni]
Melbourne ['melbɔ:n, 'melbən]
Mungingee [mʌŋɪŋgi:]
Ngarrindjeri [gɑ:'rɪndʒeri:]
Nugget ['nʌgɪt]
Pine Creek [ˌpaɪn 'kri:k]
Pingelly [pɪn'dʒeli]
Raukkan ['rəʊkæn]
Rosie ['rəʊzi]
Rusty ['rʌsti]
Tara Downs ['tɑ:rə ˌdaʊnz]
Yartooka [jɑ:'tu:kə]